❧ ❧ ❧

The
Care and
Feeding of
Indigo
Children

☙ ☙ ☙

Also by Doreen Virtue, Ph.D.

Books

MESSAGES FROM YOUR ANGELS (available April 2002)
ANGEL VISIONS II
EATING IN THE LIGHT (with Becky Prelitz, M.F.T., R.D.)
HEALING WITH THE FAIRIES
ANGEL VISIONS
*DIVINE PRESCRIPTIONS
HEALING WITH THE ANGELS
"I'D CHANGE MY LIFE IF I HAD MORE TIME"
*DIVINE GUIDANCE
CHAKRA CLEARING
ANGEL THERAPY
THE LIGHTWORKER'S WAY
CONSTANT CRAVING A–Z
CONSTANT CRAVING
THE YO-YO DIET SYNDROME
LOSING YOUR POUNDS OF PAIN

Audio Programs

ANGELS AMONG US (with Michael Toms)—available April 2002
MESSAGES FROM YOUR ANGELS
(abridged audio book—available April 2002)
PAST-LIFE REGRESSION WITH THE ANGELS
*DIVINE PRESCRIPTIONS
THE ROMANCE ANGELS
CONNECTING WITH YOUR ANGELS (2-tape set and 6-tape set)
MANIFESTING WITH THE ANGELS
KARMA RELEASING
HEALING YOUR APPETITE, HEALING YOUR LIFE
HEALING WITH THE ANGELS
*DIVINE GUIDANCE
CHAKRA CLEARING
LOSING YOUR POUNDS OF PAIN (abridged audio book)

Oracle Cards (44 divination cards and guidebook)

HEALING WITH THE ANGELS ORACLE CARDS
HEALING WITH THE FAIRIES ORACLE CARDS
MESSAGES FROM YOUR ANGELS ORACLE CARDS
(card pack and booklet) (available April 2002)

All of the above titles are available through your local bookstore.
All items except those with an asterisk (*) are available
by calling Hay House at (800) 654-5126.

Please visit the Hay House Website at: **hayhouse.com**
and Dr. Virtue's Website at **AngelTherapy.com**

The Care and Feeding of Indigo Children

Doreen Virtue, Ph.D.

Hay House, Inc.
Carlsbad, California • Sydney, Australia
Canada • Hong Kong • United Kingdom

Published and distributed in the United States by:
Hay House, Inc., P.O. Box 5100, Carlsbad, CA 92018-5100
(800) 654-5126 • (800) 650-5115 (fax) • www.hayhouse.com

Editorial supervision: Jill Kramer
Design: Highpoint, Inc., Claremont, CA

Library of Congress Cataloging-in-Publication Data

Virtue, Doreen
    The care and feeding of indigo children / Doreen Virtue.
      p. cm.
    Includes bibliographical references.
    ISBN 1-56170-846-1 (tradepaper)
      1. Children—Miscellanea. 2. Children—Care.
3. Children—Nutrition. 4. Exceptional children. 5. Color—
Psychological aspects.

RJ208.V57 2001
649'.153--dc21   2001039069

ISBN 1-56170-846-1

05 04 03 02   5 4 3 2
1st printing, August 2001
2nd printing, January 2002

Printed in Canada

❧ ❧ ❧

To my Indigo Children,
Chuck, Grant, Nicole, and Catherine.
Thank you for your Divine Love and Light!

❧ ❧ ❧

❧ Contents ❧

❧ *Foreword* ❧

by Jan Tober

In the spring of 1999, my writing partner, Lee Carroll, and I authored a book called The Indigo Children. It had to do with the concept of new kinds of children being born on the planet—a group we called "Indigo Children."

Over the last ten years, Lee and I have traveled worldwide as authors and speakers on self-empowerment and the power of love. During the last few years, the focus of our audiences, particularly among parents, caregivers, counselors, teachers, grandparents, and anyone who was directly in contact with children, was often geared to one question, which was: "What can we do to help the children?" These individuals were quite concerned about the exponential growth of the drug Ritalin and other similar drugs being prescribed and given to young people everywhere. Even preschoolers and toddlers were beginning to be treated with this drug in some states. The rise in the use of these drugs has been shocking, and there has been growing concern.

The conclusion of our book was that today's children are different—more challenging, more intelligent, more confrontational, more intuitive, more spiritual, and in some cases, even more violent (as in the case of recent school killings where children have killed children)—from any generation we have yet seen. This calls for a new and different way of parenting and schooling—outside of the old ways.

Dr. Doreen Virtue is one of the major contributing authors of our 1999 book, which is where we first introduced the term *Indigo Children* to a worldwide audience. She is a spiritual doctor of psychology and lecturer who is making a major contribution to the paradigm shift that society needs to recognize and implement.

The labels of ADD (Attention Deficit Disorder) and ADHD (Attention Deficit Hyperactive Disorder) are being thrown around liberally these days, and they've now become household phrases. In addition, the conventional ways of parenting and teaching have become outmoded and dated—some even archaic. Of all the solutions presented in the many books on the subject of ADD, ADHD, and their related drugs, there are still no conclusive answers for parents, especially at the holistic level. Doreen's work focuses on this topic and gives us positive suggestions and alternatives. Like a breath of fresh air, her approach helps us balance this issue in light of the new attributes within our young people—whom we're calling the Indigo Children.

Who are these Indigo Children now being born en masse, and how did we hear about this phenomenon? In the mid-1970s, I met a profound teacher and counselor named Nancy Ann Tappe. Nancy was researching colors of the human aura and their possible meanings as part of her ongoing studies as a therapist. In 1982, she wrote the book *Understanding Your Life Through Color.*

Nancy classified certain types of human attributes and behavioral patterns that seemed to correlate to the colors of the electromagnetic field surrounding all living things—in the case of humans, the auric field. Through much research, Nancy created what appeared to be a startlingly accurate and revealing psychological profiling system using this new auric color method—an entirely new premise for human behavior grouping. One of the new classifications noticed was a deep blue color that was being seen in about 80 percent of the children born after 1980. She called this new color "indigo"; hence, the name of our own book, and our ongoing study about these new children.

All Indigos are *not* ADD/ADHD, and all children diagnosed with these symptoms are *not* all automatically Indigos. The characteristics of the Indigo behavior, however, often seems to be interchangeable with these claimed disorders. In our book, Lee and I use this definition:

> An Indigo child is one who displays a new and unusual set of psychological attributes and shows a pattern of behavior generally undocumented before. This pattern has common, unique factors that suggest that those who interact with them (parents, in particular) change their treatment and upbringing of them in order to achieve balance. To ignore these new patterns is to potentially create imbalance and frustration in the mind of this precious new life.

We also listed some of the most common behavioral patterns of Indigos:

1. They come into the world with a feeling of royalty (and often act like it).
2. They have a feeling of "deserving to be here," and are surprised when others don't share that.
3. Self-worth is not a big issue. They often tell the parents "who they are."
4. They have difficulty with absolute authority (authority without explanation or choice).
5. They simply will not do certain things; for example, waiting in line is difficult for them.
6. They get frustrated with systems that are ritual oriented and don't require creative thought.

7. They often see better ways of doing things, both at home and in school, which makes them seem like "system busters" (nonconforming to any system).

8. They seem antisocial unless they're with their own kind. If there are no others of like consciousness around them, they often turn inward, feeling like no other human understands them. School is often extremely difficult for them socially.

9. They will not respond to "guilt" discipline ("Wait until your father gets home.")

10. They aren't shy about letting you know what they need.

As you read this book by this loving and dedicated woman, please allow your heart, as well as your mind, to open up to new possibilities for our children. Dr. Virtue bridges a gap between the linear and creative ideas that are currently available to the public. Her credentials are powerful, and her intuition is illuminating. I'm excited and delighted about her contribution.

The children are our future. Let's reframe the present reality from our heart-space, changing the potential future, and allowing us to live in a more balanced existence. Let us become the Rainbow Bridge from the old ways to the new — for our children, ourselves, and our planet.

Thank you, Doreen, for this book!

— Jan Tober, co-author of *The Indigo Children*

❧ Acknowledgments ❧

*A bouquet of thank you's to Lee Carroll, Jan Tober,
Nancy Ann Tappe, Charles Schenk, Nicole Farmer,
Steven Farmer, Grant Schenk, Michele Avanti,
Alec Bridges, Jill Kramer, Reid Tracy, Louise L. Hay,
Ron Tillinghast, and all of the Indigo Children
and their parents who contributed interviews
and stories to this book.*

❧ ❧ ❧

✤ *Introduction* ✤

Little Lightworkers

Indigo Children represent a special breed of individuals who have come to our planet to bestow us with their gifts. They're here to change our political, educational, nutritional, family, and other systems. They're also here to help all of us reach our potential by becoming more natural and more intuitive.

Like the early settlers to North America or Australia, Indigos are self-reliant, headstrong, and creative. They have a job to do, and they won't let anyone stand in their way. Earlier generations were given the intuitive message: "Change the government, heal the world." They started out in that direction but allowed apathy and family responsibilities to discourage and distract them. The Indigo Children won't let the same thing happen—unless we drug them into submission, that is.

Yet, there are some people who resent the change that these children represent. They would like the school system to remain in its present state, and they'd like the Indigo Children to comply. Since you can't force Indigo Children to do anything, and they see coercion as a form of dishonest manipulation, drugging is being used as an insidious method of making the Indigo Child "fit in."

Indigo Children are often labeled "ADD" or "ADHD," meaning that they either have Attention Deficit Disorder or Attention Deficit with Hyperactivity Disorder, respectively. But these children aren't disordered—the world they're trying to fit into is! It's filled with unnaturalness and dishonesty. And, as, Dawn, an Indigo Child who will be quoted throughout this book, put it, "Oh, we're attention-deficit-disordered, all right. We have a deficit of attention from our parents, as well as other adults whom we need help and guidance from."

In our modern world, people lie to themselves and each other, subsisting on processed food and dirty air. Each day, they go to jobs they hate and detach from their underlying feelings of discontentment. These children, on the other hand, aren't equipped with the ability to dissociate and lie to themselves. They're incredibly telepathic and have too much integrity to betray themselves. In a way, Indigo Children are healthy role models for all of us.

Perhaps ADHD actually stands for:

Attention
Dialed into a
Higher
Dimension

And, if you look at the term ADD as the word *add*, you can see that it's a synonym for *plus* and *positive*. The truth is that Indigo Children *do* have many characteristics that are positive, and they can be a plus for their family and community.

Indigo Children are built for a tough mission that will involve rebuilding our government, educational, and social systems. It's almost like they're in boot camp being prepared for combat. Indigo Children seem to require a high degree of stimulation and excitement in their lives. It's as if their brains were wired to be able to withstand high amounts of stress, and if the environment doesn't provide enough stimulation, Indigo Children seek or create it themselves.

Gifted and ADHD children share many similar characteristics, including high IQ's, creativity, and a penchant for risk-taking. In fact, experts say that the only difference between a gifted child and an ADHD child is that gifted children finish the projects they start, whereas ADHD children leave projects unfinished. Perhaps what ADHD children need, then, is guidance with respect to organizational skills . . . instead of Ritalin.

Indigo Children are young eccentrics who make their own rules and live by their hearts and wit. Yet, even this propensity has positive effects. Dr. David Weeks, of the Royal Edinburgh Hospital in Scotland, conducted interviewed with 1,100 "eccentrics." He found that they shared three primary characteristics: (1) a strong will; (2) a good sense of humor; and (3) a creative imagination. They also have fewer health problems than the general population and live longer. In addition, Dr. Weeks found that "eccentrics tend to be cheerful, idealistic, and full of projects to improve or save the world." So, there are many pluses to being eccentric.

Dr. Weeks concluded that the eccentrics "share an overriding curiosity that drives them forward and often makes them oblivious to the small irritations and stresses of daily life that plague the general population." Indigo Children and eccentrics are too busy dreaming up ways to save the world to be bothered with making their beds!

There's a story about a child who encountered a huge pile of manure. She took a shovel and began digging the manure furiously. Her mother saw this behavior and said, "My goodness! What are you doing?"

"I know that with this much manure, there must be a pony in here somewhere!" replied the little girl.

With Indigo Children, we often have to reframe their behavior and dig for the pony in the same way. So often, these children have been punished, scolded, and ridiculed—if not at home, then by teachers and peers. They develop shame about who they are. This shame tarnishes the luster on their golden gifts. Like a dog who has been beaten too much, Indigo Children often walk with their heads hanging down and their "tails" between their legs. Much of their behavioral problems stem from the trauma of shame and emotional abuse, rather than from their "ADD."

Indigo Children *know* that they're different from the majority. Many of them have told me, "I feel like a bus dropped me off on this planet, and I wonder when it's coming to pick me back up and take me home." Fortunately, there are enough Indigos alive right now so that they can form peer groups at school. Like the cliques that many of us recall

("The Jocks," "The Socialites," and so on), a new group has formed . . . and they are the Indigo Children.

This social group can form a buffer to ease the pain of being teased or reprimanded for being different. Without this social support from friends or family, sensitive Indigo Children may believe that something is wrong with them. This can lead to acting-out, or becoming highly introverted.

"ADD does not produce delinquency," says Jeffrey Freed, M.A.T., author of *Right-Brained Children in a Left-Brained World*, "but I believe the mislabeling and shaming associated with it are contributing factors. The majority of these rebellious misfits might have led happy, productive lives were it not for their 'crime' of having a different learning style."

Indigos feel old when they're born. In some ways, they know a lot more than adults, yet they have limited opportunities to express their gifts because of time and money constraints in the educational system. School and homework take up the whole day—and it doesn't pay them a dime, to boot! How would you feel if you had to go somewhere all day long, be with people who teased or shunned you, were told that something was wrong with you—and you received no money for it? Sure, you'd be told that "someday" all that work would lead to compensation, but you'd never be quite sure how that would actually occur.

A 19-year-old Indigo Child described her experiences in school and in life to me in this way:

> My name is Alicia, and that means "truthful." I live by my name. I cannot stand lies and dishonesty. When I'm in school, I can't listen. I know that there's no point learning what they're trying to teach me because I'm never going to use it in the future.

> I know that there's a purpose for me on this earth. I know that for sure, but I don't know what it is. I know that I'm supposed to help people, but I don't know who or how. I know there's something bigger, and it has to do with my soul, not my knowledge in school.
>
> I can lose myself in the world so easily, but something always brings me right back, and I know it's the angels. I know that they're guarding me because they show me a thousand times a day. I've seen and felt angels, and I know when they're there. I want to tell my friends and family these things that I know, but they don't understand.

Indigos are highly creative children, and they think outside of the box. This thinking style has created many of the world's breakthrough inventions. Yet, if it's not understood and properly channeled, the Indigo's brilliance may lead to a diagnosis of ADD or ADHD. Many researchers believe that Einstein, Edison, da Vinci, and other great thinkers would have been labeled ADD were they alive today. Of course, knowing what we do about them now, we would certainly not have wanted these brilliant scientists and philosophers to have been thwarted in their meaningful work.

And *meaning* is the key to working with your Indigo Child. My work as a spiritual counselor has convinced me that every psychological malady always boils down to one thing: The person isn't working on their Divine Life Purpose. Just because your child is, well, a child, doesn't mean that he or she doesn't have existential angst. These days, children begin questioning the meaning of life at very young ages. Perhaps you did, too.

Although Indigos learn and act differently, it doesn't mean that they're less intelligent. Dr. Jane Healy, author of *Endangered Minds,* states that IQ scores are up among students today, as compared to prior generations of students.

These Indigo Children are no dummies! It's just that their overall IQ score reflects a shift, with higher scores in non-verbal intelligence ratings, and a dip in the verbal skills department. But, since IQ ratings are derived from combining nonverbal and verbal skills, the overall ranking is higher today than ever before.

However, you may not see evidence of the Indigo Children's intelligence in their report card. Instead, their brilliance shines through in high scores on video games, in creating gorgeous beaded necklaces, or memorizing every word to their favorite songs. In this book, we'll discuss ways to transfer that intelligence to other life areas, such as school and family relationships.

Indigo Children are a group of individuals who first arrived on this planet in the late 1970s. Some of them came earlier as the "explorer" Indigo Children. The earliest Indigo Children arrived in small groups in the late 1950s and 1960s to scope out the planet for the larger group that would follow.

As you read about these Indigo Children, you may find that you relate to their characteristics. You may even wonder, *Could I be an Indigo Child even though I'm a full-grown adult?* If such thoughts occur to you as you read this book, it's because you're connecting with that part of the Indigo scenario that overlaps with your Life Purpose. You, like the Indigo Children, are a *lightworker.*

Why Are They Called Indigo Children?

The term *Indigo Children* refers to the color "indigo blue," which is a deep shade of blue similar to that found in lapis stones or denim jeans. The term is derived from *chakra,* or energy, colors. Each generation seems to have a group consciousness—a group purpose, if you will. We can relate each generation's adult years to an issue and a correlated chakra, along with its corresponding color.

For instance, those in the post–Depression and post–World War II eras of the 1940s and 1950s had issues of *security*. They married young and stayed at their jobs for a lifetime. Happiness in their marriage or career was secondary to the security afforded by their stations. This type of outlook is akin to the "root chakra," which is an energy center located at the base of the spine.

Each chakra spins at a different rate, according to what issues are assigned to that chakra. The chakras assigned to material issues spin at a slower rate than the more spiritually focused chakras.

As you may know, when light moves slowly, it is perceived as the "warm colors," such as red, orange, and yellow. The faster that light waves move, the more cool their colors are. Purple is the highest-speed color, and is also associated with the most spiritual of frequencies.

The 1950s generation, associated with the root chakra, could be called "the children of the red ray." That's because the root chakra spins so slowly, and it appears to be the slowest of all light-speed colors: red.

In the 1960s and '70s, young people were less concerned with security and more interested in exploring the physical pleasures associated with drugs, sex, and rock-and-roll. These experiences correlate to the second chakra, known as the "sacral chakra." Since this chakra spins at a slightly faster rate than the root chakra, its color appears orange. You could, therefore, call young people of the '60s and '70s "children of the second—or orange—ray."

The next generation, those of the 1980s, were concerned with acquiring personal property and power. Women started to wear masculine business suits with shoulder pads. Young people acquired debt galore and bought property and cars to impress their neighbors. This behavior is associated with the third, or "solar plexus," chakra, which spins at a yellow color.

The early 1990s saw a spiritual revolution begin, with many people joining churches and temples, and reading books on nonreligious affiliated spirituality. The Pope gave a public speech apologizing for the Church's past abuses. There was also a reduction in violent crime in America. Was this spiritual interest and repentance due to the pending new millennium, which some people prophesied might be the "Second Coming"?

Whether the spiritual awakening stemmed from fear or love, it seemed to have a lasting effect. This renewed interest in spirituality has been a heart-centered process associated with the heart chakra, which spins at an emerald-green color.

The late 1990s heralded a time when many people strove to become independent. Whether it was through playing the stock market, working for oneself, or dropping out of the rat race entirely, it was a time of individualism. Downsizing at corporations meant an end to lifelong job security. Instead, it was "every man or woman for him- or herself." In addition, many people expressed a desire to bring their lives into integrity. This meant leaving situations (jobs, marriages, and so on) that didn't feel healthy. They often began entrepreneurial ventures based upon their passions. These changes are associated with the throat chakra, which works on "truth and integrity" issues in communication. This chakra spins at a color of light sky-blue.

Springboarding from the spiritual revolution of the 1990s, there was a resurgence of interest in psychic phenomena that ushered in the new millennium. For the first time, the mainstream press gave front-page coverage to psychic mediums such as James Van Praagh, John Edward, Sylvia Browne, and yours truly. Movies such as *The Sixth Sense* and television shows such as *Touched by an Angel* openly dealt with angels, Earthbound spirits, and life-after-death. This interest in psychic phenomena is regulated by the sixth chakra, known as the "third eye." This chakra spins at three different colors: white, purple, and primarily *indigo*.

Children who were born in the mid-1970s through the present day are often called Indigo Children because they are, literally, "children of the indigo ray." They are highly psychic, and they take their psychic visions and knowingness for granted. Their spiritual gifts are so highly attuned that they're often gifted (although they may think of it as cursed) in other life areas as well.

For example, many Indigo Children are artistically gifted. This isn't surprising, since artistry is a function of the right side of the brain, and Indigo Children are right-brain dominant. Their gifts are in the creation, rather than the left-brain study, of the arts. So, Indigo Children may flunk music classes because they can't memorize musical scales, but after school, they might compose the most beautiful music at home on their musical instruments, using their inner senses. In the same way, Indigos may doodle instead of listening to their teacher's lecture. But take a look at the child's doodling, and you'll often discover intricately detailed artwork.

A lot of Indigo Children are emotionally gifted as well. They often act as "street-corner psychologists" to other children, lending sympathetic ears and wise advice. People pour out their hearts to Indigo Children because of their open-heartedness and nonjudgmental nature. So, your Indigo Child may come home with a collection of rag-tag friends, who really are your "psychologist" child's caseload of clients.

Sensitive to a Fault

Indigo Children are exquisitely sensitive in many ways. They may have been subject to taunts such as "You're too sensitive," yet their sensitivity is a spiritual gift equivalent to a detecting instrument. Recall for a moment how sensitive, exposed, or aware you felt after a profound experience such as having a full-body massage or after taking a psychic development course.

Didn't you find that you were super-aware of other people's thoughts and feelings afterward, and that you needed to shield yourself from, or avoid, harsh circumstances such as crowds or angry people? Well, Indigo Children feel this way *all of the time*. They're highly aware of others' thoughts and feelings, and their sensitivity is attuned to two main areas:

1. Truth and integrity. As if they've assimilated the lessons of the generation before them, Indigo Children are exquisitely sensitive to lies or any type of lack of integrity in others. They have what author Sam Keen calls a "spiritual B.S. detector" inside their guts. You cannot lie to an Indigo Child without consequences. The child will call you on the lie, and act-out through either aggression or isolation.

This sensitivity is related to the Indigo Children's remarkable psychic abilities, and is a huge part of their Life Purpose, as you'll soon read. And part of *our* Life Purpose, as parents and teachers of Indigo Children, is to make sure that this group of "little lightworkers" holds on to their spiritual gifts, and that they're directed toward their Life Purpose.

2. Environmental toxins. Indigo Children are "natural children in an unnatural world." Many of them are experiencing their first lifetime on planet Earth, and their immune systems (physically and emotionally) aren't able to assimilate the earthly toxins in food, water, air, toiletries, cleaning supplies, artificial lighting, and relationships. Scientists have discovered huge links between ADHD and environmental toxins.

What You'll Find in This Book

This is not just another, "How to Heal ADD Naturally" book. I've read dozens of those books, and I find that they offer a great deal of relevant and scientifically sound material. Yet, each time I read an ADD self-help book, I ask myself the same question: "If this is the answer, why are Ritalin prescriptions continuing to skyrocket?" After all, the United States prescribes more Ritalin than any other country, and one in 36 boys is now on Ritalin in New South Wales, Australia. I've noticed that a lot of the ADD self-help books offer hundreds of wonderful suggestions about dietary changes and behavioral modification models. Yet, if I were a parent of a young, hyperactive Indigo Child, I would feel overwhelmed. To have a doctor tell me, "If you'll just follow these 435 tips, your child's hyperactivity will diminish," would be enough to make me quit before I even get started.

While I was researching and writing this book, my guides and angels continually reminded me to keep it simple. They said to write a book about the core issues surrounding Indigos, ADD, and ADHD—and to provide simple and realistic solutions.

While traveling around the world talking with Indigo Children and their parents, I constantly heard requests for practical answers. For instance, it's common knowledge that diet affects hyperactivity, yet many parents told me that they found changing their child's diet nearly impossible. "How am I supposed to change my child's diet when they're constantly being tempted with junk food by their friends, by TV commercials, and by fast-food outlets at school and on every corner?" parents would ask me in frustration. They want answers that they can immediately apply to their kids' lives, which will work on an everyday basis.

Perhaps like you, I'm a practical and pragmatic person, always on the lookout for what works. I'm the daughter of a Christian Science practitioner, and I witnessed miraculous healings to emotional and physical problems throughout my childhood. Mom often applied her spiritual healing to my brother and me, so I experienced them firsthand. This was in the 1960s, before "alternative healing" was popular. So, I remember being teased at school whenever I'd discuss our family's unusual beliefs and practices.

I had my two sons, Chuck and Grant, when I was in my early 20s. Chuck (my oldest, now 23 years old) was a very active boy from the first time he moved around in my womb. He hit the ground running when he was born, and he was always touching and exploring his environment. Although he was a handful, he was also extremely helpful. When he was just three years old, for instance, I wanted to make some fresh-squeezed orange juice, but I couldn't figure out how to assemble our old-fashioned and complicated juicing machine.

Half out of desperation, I asked Chuck if he could help me. He immediately went over to the machine and put it together!

As a young child, Chuck would also discuss esoteric topics with me. He'd tell me his theories about God and the size of the universe. He'd bring up these discussions out-of-the-blue, during ordinary circumstances. How I wish I'd tape-recorded his profound words!

Grant (now age 21) is also very spiritually minded and helpful, but he's quieter, more laid-back, and more introspective than Chuck. Grant and Chuck represent the two main types of Indigo Children: the aggressive warrior and the quiet artist.

When the boys were still young, I returned to college to earn my degrees in psychology. I worked as a secretary during the day and took classes during my lunch hours and in the evenings. It took a long time, but I eventually emerged with a B.A., M.A., and Ph.D. in counseling psychology.

My first counseling job was in an addictions hospital, working with drug addicts and alcoholics. I later specialized in treating people with eating disorders and opened my own clinic. During that time, I wrote self-help books about my clinical experiences. I never forgot my earlier teachings in the spiritual healing arts, yet I feared talking about them openly.

In the meantime, my guides and angels pressured me to publicly talk about my knowledge of spiritual healing. They reminded me that my Life Purpose was to teach mind-body-spirit topics. They said that every person has a Life Purpose—a mission that helps others—and that if we aren't working on our Purpose, happiness and health evade us.

But I remembered the teasing and taunting I suffered as

a child whenever I'd openly discuss our family's spiritual healing practices. I wasn't about to risk my professional reputation, my income, or a wounded ego just to talk about my spiritual beliefs! So, I ignored my angels' guidance.

It took a brush with death before I came around. I had become so accustomed to ignoring my angels (who talk to us through our intuition or inner knowing), that I was almost killed! It happened on July 15, 1995: I was getting ready to leave for an appointment in Anaheim, California, about an hour away from my coastal Orange County home. One of my angels clearly told me that if I didn't put the top up on my convertible car, it would be stolen. As was my custom at that time in my life, I ignored my angel. An hour later, two armed men held me up in a carjacking attempt.

Fortunately, my angel was still with me. He told me to resist the carjackers and to scream with all my might. For the first time in decades, I followed my angel's guidance, and I was able to escape without losing my car, purse, or life. After the incident, I was considerably traumatized, so I turned to my spiritual healing background for help. The results were miraculous, and I was healed of all post-traumatic anxiety.

That incident changed my life forever, personally and professionally. I rededicated myself to my spiritual pursuits and came out of the spiritual "closet." I stopped practicing traditional psychotherapy and began conducting "Angel Therapy" instead. Although my background is metaphysical Christianity, I began working nondenominationally with people of all religious and nonreligious backgrounds. I found that everyone with whom I worked exhibited remarkable effects in response to my "Angel Therapy." I began teaching other therapists and medical professionals how to conduct Angel

Therapy, too, and they also reported miraculous results with themselves and their clients.

I've met people who have used Angel Therapy to heal themselves and their clients of terminal, chronic, acute, and short-term physical and psychological issues. I have personally been healed of all cravings for sugar and chocolate through Angel Therapy. In this book, we'll apply Angel Therapy to the ADD and ADHD symptoms that often appear in Indigo Children. As you'll discover, Angel Therapy is wonderfully effective with these kids.

Recently, a woman named Josie approached me at my workshop with tears in her eyes and her arms outstretched, waiting to embrace me. She exclaimed that after reading my books about working with angels, she'd experienced a Divine intervention with her 13-year-old son, Chris.

"Chris was out of control before I began working with his angels," Josie explained to me. "He wouldn't come home on time, and he was using drugs. His schoolwork was a mess. Then my aunt brought home one of your books, and I read how to talk to Chris's angels. I really didn't believe in angels at the time. I thought they were like Santa Claus: a myth. But I was desperate to help my son, so I gave it a try.

"I silently talked to Chris's guardian angels, even though I wasn't really sure I was doing it right. I wasn't even sure that he had angels, the way he was acting like a devil and all! But I saw results almost immediately. I kept talking to those angels every night."

I asked Josie how Chris was doing these days.

"He's great!" she beamed. "He's happy, off drugs, and he's doing well in school."

❧ ❧ ❧

Over the years, I've found that the most effective and down-to-earth healing methods are spiritually based. If you're saying to yourself, "Only a miracle could help my child," you're right.

If you're an Indigo Child reading this book, I'm so happy! You obviously care about yourself and your Life Purpose. I'll teach you the same methods I've used with my clients and audience members to help *them* discover their Purpose. Once you find your Purpose and begin working on it, much of the inner emptiness and pain goes away. I'll also teach you some spiritual healing methods to help you clear yourself of the negative energy you may absorb from other people. These practices can help you feel more energetic, develop greater peace of mind, and enable you to sleep and focus better.

Indigo Children are here to usher in the New Age of Peace. It's our spiritual duty to help them in any way we can!

✥✥✥ ✥✥✥

✨ *Chapter One* ✨

Am I, or Is My Child, an Indigo?

An Indigo Child is usually an individual with the following characteristics:

1. Strong-willed
2. Born in 1978 or later
3. Headstrong
4. Creative, with an artistic flair for music, jewelry making, poetry, etc.
5. Prone to addictions
6. An "old soul," as if they're 13, going on 43
7. Intuitive or psychic, possibly with a history of seeing angels or deceased people
8. An isolationist, either through aggressive acting-out, or through fragile introversion
9. Independent and proud, even if they're constantly asking you for money

10. Possesses a deep desire to help the world in a big way
11. Wavers between low self-esteem and grandiosity
12. Bores easily
13. Has probably been diagnosed as having ADD or ADHD
14. Prone to insomnia, restless sleep, nightmares, or difficulty/fear of falling asleep
15. Has a history of depression, or even suicidal thoughts or attempts
16. Looks for real, deep, and lasting friendships
17. Easily bonds with plants or animals

When I list these characteristics of Indigo Children at my workshops, most parents and kids quickly "get it," and know for sure that they or their children are Indigos. But I still receive questions from people who want to absolutely know. The answer is that Indigos are as varied as there are shades of the color blue. We *need* variety among Indigos, who will assume diverse roles in the New Age of Peace. Some will be leaders; others will be researchers, healers, supporters, or teachers.

Yet, if your children responded positively to 14 or more of the above characteristics, then they're most likely Indigos. If they related to between 11 and 13 of the above characteristics, they're probably "Indigos in training," or those who are just developing their "little lightworker" traits. These descriptions could also apply to Indigo Children who are being artificially detached from their spiritual gifts, through the use of authoritative force and/or Ritalin.

If you're an adult who relates to the above characteristics, it's possible that you were one of the first forerunners of the Indigo Children. A few Indigos came to Earth, long before 1978, to gather information and set the groundwork for the coming of the Indigo Children race. Most likely, though, if you're an adult who relates to the concept of being an Indigo Child, you are instead what we call a "lightworker." My book *The Lightworker's Way* (Hay House, 1997) may offer some insights for you on your personal path.

In the next few chapters, we'll discuss why the Indigo Children have these unique characteristics, what their purpose is, and how adults can help Indigos in their daily lives.

❧ ❧ ❧ ❧ ❧ ❧

✨ *Chapter Two* ✨

ADD, ADHD, and Ritalin

When Indigo Children are labeled with Attention Deficit Disorder (ADD) or Attention Deficit with Hyperactivity Disorder (ADHD), their inner feelings of being "different" are validated. But instead of feeling happy that they're unique because of their Life Purpose and spiritual gifts, Indigo Children feel ashamed of their differences.

It's estimated that more than six million American children now take psychotropic medication for ADHD, depression, and other psychological maladies. As I mentioned earlier, one in every 36 Australian boys in New South Wales takes Ritalin, which is the most widely prescribed medication for children. Other commonly prescribed drugs include Dexedrine, Cylert, Tofranil, Norpamin, Prozac, and Paxil.

Being put on medication is a two-fold dilemma for Indigo Children. On the one hand, it offers them the opportunity to finally "fit in" with other kids and to please their parents and teachers. It may even give them a "high" that helps them escape the pain of feeling different, or feeling empty inside if they aren't working on their Purpose. But the price is high: Their spiritual gifts will be bound in a chemical strait-jacket.

Indigo Children who take Ritalin or other psychotropic drugs soon lose touch with their intuition, psychic abilities, and warrior personality. These children were sent to Earth with these three spiritual gifts for the express purpose of cleaning up our planet, environmentally and socially. When we turn Indigo Children into apathetic conformists through prescription drugs, they forget their Life Purpose. This leads to one more generation where society, particularly the environment, becomes sicker and more polluted.

Yes, Ritalin does work to harness a wild child's behavior temporarily, but the child must then stay on the drugs for their effects to last. There are many other answers to the temporary behavioral problems of children who are labeled ADD or ADHD. These solutions are natural, and most of them are free of charge or are available at a low cost. They will help your children sleep, concentrate, and get along with others better. And most important, these natural methods will enhance instead of hinder your Indigo Children's Purpose and spiritual gifts.

I've done my best in this book to give you some basic, easy-to-do, practical solutions. I know that if I gave you a laundry list of "do this, that, this, and that" suggestions, you'd become overwhelmed. After all, studies show that ADD and ADHD run in families. Children who are ADD- or ADHD-labeled are likely to have parents who exhibit ADD or ADHD behaviors, such as disorganization, hyperactivity, or impulsivity.

What this means to us, in reality, is that most Indigo Children are being raised by lightworkers, and they share some of the same characteristics of being "ungrounded" and "disorganized" on this dense Earthly plane. So, it's easy for the lightworker parents to become overwhelmed by complicated suggestions about naturally healing ADHD or ADD behavior. Truly, if you apply just half of this book's suggestions, you and your Indigo will experience positive results.

If That Wasn't Bad Enough . . .

Not only do Indigo Children lose sight of their spiritual gifts and Purpose, but Indigos who use prescription medication have a high likelihood of using illegal drugs. Perhaps it's because those who experience anxiety or depression are seeking relief. Or, maybe it's because we're teaching our children to "just say yes to drugs" when we send them to the school nurse's office for their daily dose of Ritalin.

Ritalin is sold on the street and at schools as a feel-good drug. Since it provides a similar high to that of cocaine or speed, this shouldn't come as a surprise. Ritalin has also been linked to violent behavior, according to the International Narcotics Control Board. Some experts believe that the shootings at Columbine and other schools were precipitated by the Ritalin and other psychotropic drugs reportedly being taken by the kids who did the shooting.

Mary Ann Block, author of *No More Ritalin*, says:

> I believe children want to learn, and most have the ability to learn. Most of the children I see in my office are very bright. But they often have trouble learning. It is our responsibility as adults and educators to help each child learn

the best way she can without giving her stimulants and other types of drugs.

If a child cannot sit down at a piano and innately know how to play it, we don't call him or her learning disabled and prescribe medications. We teach the child how to play by giving lessons, time to practice, and years to become accomplished. But if that same child cannot immediately learn how to read or write or do math, we call him or her learning disabled.

Bonnie Cramond, Ph.D., a researcher who has studied the similarities between creativity and ADHD behaviors, writes:

> Michael Kearney, the youngest college graduate in the world, was diagnosed as a toddler with ADHD and prescribed Ritalin. However, his parents declined drug treatment and decided to nurture Michael's genius with education instead.
>
> He started school at age three, entered junior college at six, and graduated from the University of South Alabama at ten. His father, Kevin Kearney, refused the notion that Michael's inattention is due to a lack of attention: In fact, children like Michael have an attention surplus. He's so much faster than we are. In two seconds he has figured out what you're going to say. He has toyed with a few answers and now he's looking around waiting for you to finish. It looks like he's not paying attention and it drives teachers crazy.

Indigo Children Speak Out Against Drugs

In this book, you'll not only read about what experts and the angels say about Indigo Children and their ADHD symptoms, but you'll read what the Indigo Children themselves think and feel. In my review of the current books dealing with "healing ADHD naturally," I never found any featuring interviews with the kids themselves. It was always the "experts" telling us how the kids felt.

So, I asked an Indigo Child, my stepdaughter Nicole, to conduct interviews with Indigo Children. I knew that kids would open up to another young person easier than they would to an adult. My hunch was correct. You'll read the transcripts of these interviews with the Indigo Children here, and you'll see that they reveal their deepest emotions to her.

For instance, here is what several Indigo Children had to say about Ritalin and other psychotropic medications:

> **Alec:** People should learn how to take care of their problems without a drug or else it will come up in some way or another later. When they stop taking the drug, they're not going to know how to deal with the problem that's being suppressed. I know one guy who took Ritalin when he was a kid, and now he's a heroin addict.
>
> People with ADD come up with good ideas, and maybe they aren't in the right environment. Or, they need to practice meditating so that they can build their concentration abilities. Most people with ADD are multitaskers. Everyone thinks you should stick to one thing, but there are some people who can work on a lot of projects and still get them done.
>
> **Hunter:** I've known people who have taken Ritalin, and it mellowed them out, but it gave them the chance to get into other, stronger drugs. I think if every kid had someone tell them that they were fine and exactly what they were doing was totally normal and natural, then they'd get through it in their own way. It would be a lot easier than saying that there's a drug that's going to do it.
>
> **Dawn:** I think Ritalin is ridiculous. Adults try to put their kids in categories to make themselves feel safe. I've seen it happen a lot of times. Just so they can push it off on something else. "Oh, well, they have ADD, so that's why they're

like this." That's giving an excuse for it. Oftentimes it's misprescribed, and it has really messed with a lot of kids. A lot of times Attention Deficit Disorder is from lack of attention from the parent. Not giving the kid attention—I think that's where a lot of the acting-out and loud behavior comes from.

I've seen how Ritalin can make kids become depressed and totally unlike themselves. There have been thousands of cases of suicides on Ritalin. I don't see it as being a positive thing at all. I've heard people say that it's really helped their kid and their kid is doing so much better, but how are they doing better when they're on a drug to make them how the parent wants the kid to be? That's not healthy at all.

I think parents put their kids on Ritalin because they don't know how to fix the problem with their kids, or they don't want to put in the energy to do so, so they take the easy way out. I think this world is pretty programmed into thinking that prescription pills are the way to fix things.

Elizabeth: Before a friend of mine began taking Ritalin, he was much more full of life and energy and vibrant. When he was on Ritalin, he was drowsy. He wasn't moody, but he just wasn't in a good mood. He was toned down; his emotions were toned down. When talking to him, he wasn't as present. When he was off of Ritalin, he was very interested in things. I think he was so much more himself, much happier, and more beautiful without Ritalin.

Adam: When I was in the third grade, I knew a kid who had ADD or ADHD, and he was on Ritalin. He didn't really have any moods when he was on it. He just listened and didn't really talk. I don't think Ritalin should be prescribed, because it zones you out and you don't want to do anything. I think drugs are a short-term answer to a long-term problem.

David: I've never taken Ritalin, but I have taken Zoloft and Paxil. I got off of Zoloft because it made me sleep too much and I would miss my classes at school. And I got off of Paxil because of night sweats. That stuff is evil. Paxil is supposed to make you less self-conscious and let you go out and be a part of society with less fear and less panic attacks. What it did for me is it got rid of my mental problems, but it gave me different problems that made me even more fearful.

I think that the only reason that parents put their kids on Ritalin is because they don't want to deal with them. It's like a horse that's out of control. If you really want the horse to be a good horse, then you have to train it, take care of it, put all of your energy into it, and then it will be a horse that will give back to you. If you just give it tranquilizers, then when it wakes up, it's going to be more out of control. I know so many kids who get addicted to other drugs when they're put on Ritalin. If a parent puts their kid on Ritalin, then the parents are just taking an easy way out. There's no excuse. If a kid is hyperactive, then find something for him or her to do, like art or something, and they'll probably be calmer after that.

Chris: I think that in our "pharmaceutical" society, we have drugs for things like baldness and impotence instead of drugs for serious diseases like malaria. We just try to cure cosmetic things too much. It's the same with the natural medicine thing, too. If you have an ailment, then you take a natural pill—but a pill, nonetheless—for it. I don't think that this is the way to solve the problem. Instead of fixing the deep problem, we just coat it over. It's like a breath mint. I think that's a big problem with our society. Instead of fixing the cause, we just try to mask it.

Ryan: I hate Ritalin. Ritalin got me liking the thought of doing speed. Up to that point, I was on Prozac and those kinds of drugs, and they didn't work at all. I didn't have any energy, and as I think back, well, maybe the reason I didn't have any energy was because they were giving me all these drugs I don't need.

When I got put on Prozac, I'd gone to this doctor I'd never met and saw him for a half hour and he put me on Prozac, and at the time I thought it was kind of cool. That's when it was kind of big, and I had just done a report on it, and I read how people don't like their personality and take this stuff and it makes them the complete opposite. I thought it was so cool because I wouldn't recognize myself. But I took it, and it really made me feel worse. They would tell me, "You have this thing (depression), but don't worry about it; you're not any different."

Telling me I'm not different, but knowing that I had this thing, made me feel I had an excuse to screw off. So, I screwed off, and then they put me on Ritalin. I took the ADD test, and I didn't have it. But I seemed a little distracted. I'm not hyperactive, but distracted, so they put me on it, and the first day I took it I thought, *Whoa, this stuff makes you feel like a spaz.*

I was doing home study at the time, and I did a week's homework in one day. My parents thought it was great. But then it goes away and you feel like death, like you're going to kill yourself. So I started taking too much of it, and that really screws with your body chemistry. I read that the average animal, after its heart beats 800 million times, dies. I was thinking, *This stuff makes my heart beat three times as fast; this must not be too good for me.* Speeding up my heart rate. I found out that it was pretty much speed.

After about a month of doing Ritalin, I was really lethargic, and it didn't help me with homework anymore. I pretty much turned into a zombie. Nobody recognized me. I had friends at school who I stopped talking to. I couldn't even stand being myself. After I got off of Ritalin, I started doing speed because I liked the whole feeling. It pisses me off that I was ever given Ritalin because, for what?

I was 15, and you know what? All kids have trouble at 15. I think Ritalin is a terrible drug. Kids are thrown on that like antibiotics for a cold. And now I see kids being put on it at age six or seven, or even earlier.

I think adults give Ritalin to kids because it's an easy way out, an alternative to parenting your kids, and to dealing with the real issue. I think a lot of parents don't really know what Ritalin is and what it does. It's a drug, it gets you high, then you become addicted. Once your body is addicted to something, it opens that door to addiction. Once you open that door to addiction, it's so hard to get rid of it. It's impossible; it will always be there.

❧❧❧

Gabrielle Zale, an art and music therapist who has successfully helped kids with ADHD symptoms through her creativity projects, says, "I have seen these children medicated heavily, which is just the opposite of what they need. I have also seen these children beg not to be medicated, and the system medicated them anyway."

This book is not necessarily anti-Ritalin, but it does strongly suggest natural, healthful, life-enhancing, and low-cost alternatives to help you and your child regain a sense of family unity and peace of mind. My prayer is that you'll read this entire book, share it with your Indigo Children, and try some or all of the methods described.

❧❧❧ ❧❧❧

✿ Chapter Three ✿

The Purpose of Indigo Children

Every individual has a Life Purpose. This is the mission that you agreed to prior to your incarnation. There are two parts to your Purpose: a personal one and a global one. Your personal Purpose involves a particular characteristic that you're trying to develop in this life, such as patience or compassion. Your global Purpose involves discovering, developing, and using your natural talents and interests to help other people and the planet.

Some people have a Purpose that just affects a few, while others are spiritually contracted to help thousands of people. Just like in an orchestra, every player is equally important. Both the piccolo player and the first violinist are crucial to the music's orchestration.

In the same way, God and the world are counting on you to remember and work on your Life Purpose. Deep down, you probably know that you're here to make the world a better place. If you feel that you're not doing so, your inner self begins to nudge you. This nudging can take the form of anxiety or a sense of time urgency. If you ignore the inner nudging, you may begin to feel empty or depressed. If you believe that others are blocking your urgings, you may blame them and feel angry or ripped off. If you feel unqualified to help the world, you may collapse into low self-esteem.

Each person has a global Life Purpose and a personal mission. The global mission is the overarching, or umbrella-like Purpose that you're engaged in. Your personal mission is the specific form that your Life Purpose is to take.

Indigo Children all share a similar global Life Purpose: to help usher in the New Age of Peace. Here's how Hunter Zinkle, a 21-year-old Indigo Child, puts it, "I know that my purpose is to help the human existence run a little smoother. I try to do my best with everyone I come in contact with, to help their lives seem a little easier and less convoluted. With a lot of my friends, I feel like I'm opening the flower of life for them. With other friends, it seems like I'm their guide to life."

Hunter is a happy and well-adjusted Indigo Child because he knows his Purpose and is actively working on it. He knows that you don't have to wait until you get paid money for your Purpose before you begin it.

In the following section, I'll delve into the spiritual and scientific principles behind one's Life Purpose. Then we'll take steps so that your Indigo Children can more specifically discover what their personal mission entails.

Helping your children understand what their mission is helps them fill up the emptiness that comes from feeling like they don't matter. Most Indigos have received plenty of messages that they're "weird," "don't fit in," "are disordered," "are bad," "lazy," "not really trying," or "crazy." Their self-esteem has taken a real beating by the time they reach adolescence. Yet, despite this form of abuse perpetrated by teachers, parents, and/or other school kids, Indigos still feel compelled to help others. What they need, usually, is some guidance on how to channel their altruism.

The Roots of the Indigo Child's Purpose

The role of Indigo Children in the world today has ancient roots. It begins with a land called "Lemuria," which once existed in the Pacific Rim. The Hawaiian islands are remnants of Lemuria, which was a lush, tropical paradise. The Lemurians ate the exotic fruit that grew naturally on the islands without having to worry about getting food each day. Perhaps because the people didn't have to compete for their sustenance, they were peaceful and loving, and they communicated telepathically with each other.

Intuitively, the Lemurians got the message that their land was sinking. They quietly and peacefully began walking westward to the regions that now form the Pacific coast of North America. Others went to higher ground, to the area that is now occupied by the islands of Hawaii. Because they followed their inner guidance, the Lemurians escaped the mass deaths precipitated by Earth changes.

The Lemurians continued their peaceful existence as natives of the areas now known as Canada, the United States, and Mexico. When settlers from Europe arrived, they began teaching the generations descended from Lemurians some new and unnatural skills, which included relying on spoken and written language instead of nonverbal communication, eating processed foods, inhumanely raising and slaughtering animals, and basing their spirituality on externals such as a separated God, religious rules, and ancient texts. As the

Lemurians adapted these unnatural practices, they lost many of their spiritual abilities.

The world became more unnaturally based. Soon, science began doubting spirituality and related gifts. "Anything that you can't touch, see, or measure doesn't exist!" science proclaimed. Spirituality became an industrialized business in the form of organized religions, and some of them lost touch with their original spiritual bases and instead focused on controlling the masses. One of the largest organized religions even put people to death if they acted outside of church rules.

The fear of death or ostracism made many people comply with religious authority. They surrendered their own ability to talk to God, and instead relied on high-ranking members of their church or temple as their avenue for receiving Divine messages. The religious leaders said that God was angry and vengeful, and that the people must follow His rules or suffer the punishment. So, they naturally complied.

From time to time, though, spiritual renaissances would occur. In the last days of the 20th century, many people opened themselves up to spiritual and/or religious concepts. Some of this behavior was sparked by a fear that the year 2000 was a time of spiritual reckoning, or the prophesied "Second Coming." Many people attending my workshops at that time told me, "I don't really believe that the year 2000 will bring about the apocalypse, but I'm getting my spiritual life in order *just in case*."

Fortunately, many scientists embarked on a study of spirituality and related topics during that time. Research on the effect of prayer on healing poured in from every leading university, and the studies tended to show positive correlations between the two concepts.

Quantum physicists also started to delve into the role of human consciousness and how it affected matter. For instance, these scientists discovered that whatever a person is thinking while peering through an electronic microscope affects the motion of the electrons under that device.

Other scientists began doing research on humans' psychic abilities. Nearly everyone has a story to tell of some psychic phenomenon that has occurred in their life that they can't explain. Well, one scientist named Daryl Bem decided that all of the studies conducted on telepathy up to that point had been faulty. For one thing, the previous scientists were prejudiced in favor of proving psychic abilities, and their beliefs unfairly influenced the study outcomes, Bem said. A Ph.D. in engineering at Cornell University in New York, Bem decided to create the most tightly controlled study on telepathy ever done in order to disprove the notion of psychic abilities.

So, between 1983 and 1989, Bem took 240 randomly selected Cornell students and put them in two soundproof, isolated rooms. He asked one group of students to look at random pictures and to mentally project these images to the students in the other room. The other students were instructed to reveal whatever mental pictures they "saw," and researchers would compare those mental pictures to those that the other group was "sending" to them. Bem fully expected that his study would show no correlation between the pictures that were sent and those that were mentally received.

He was surprised when the results showed a statistically significant correlation between the pictures sent and received! So, Bem conducted the entire experiment again, using different students. But again, the results showed that the mental pictures "received" by the students matched the ones that had been sent from across campus. Bem conducted the experiment 11 times before conceding that there was significant evidence to support the existence of telepathy.

Other pioneering scientists who are helping us accept telepathy and other spiritual gifts as "normal "human behaviors," include Dr. Dean Radin, formerly with the University of Nevada, Las Vegas. Radin has conducted a number of studies showing the invisible thread that connects us all, and which allows us to telepathically communicate with other people.

One of the most fascinating studies conducted by Radin involved two men who didn't know each other. One man (Man A) had a blood pressure monitor on him. The other man (Man B) was in a separate room, out of earshot. Man B was told to think a loving thought about Man A. At that exact moment, Man A immediately registered a drop in blood pressure. Then, Man B was told to think an angry thought about Man A. Immediately, Man A's blood pressure soared, although he had no idea of the basis for the experiment. His mind wasn't consciously aware that Man B was thinking loving or angry thoughts about him, but his body knew. This same experiment was replicated, with the same results (using heart rate instead of blood pressure, though) in Japan.

So, telepathy may be a form of nonverbal communication based on the body's inner ears. Apparently, our body is sensitive to thought waves, although our conscious mind often tunes them out.

Telepathic Indigo Children

Virtually every parent, teacher, and health-care professional I've interviewed has said that they notice how "today's kids" are incredibly psychic. The Indigo Children with whom I've interacted report seeing angels, auras, fairies, and deceased loved ones. They can feel the integrity level of a stranger immediately, and they sense when they're being lied to. Also, these children stand by their psychic impressions instead of doubting them.

For instance, I'll ask Indigo Children, "How do you know if angels are real?" and they'll laugh and say, "Because I know that they are! I can see them!" Then I'll ask them, "What do you want to say to adults who don't believe in angels?" As if on cue, the Indigos always answer, "They *should* believe in angels, because they're real, and because they'll help make your life much better!" (I'll discuss this particular spiritual gift of Indigo Children in further detail later in the book.)

A researcher named William MacDonald at the University of Ohio found that children had the highest number of *verifiable* psychic experiences, compared to other age groups. Why is this? For one thing, children have a lot less stress and fewer worries. But my experiences have also shown me that a key element in Indigo Children's psychic ability is their refusal to concern themselves with whether their psychic impressions are real or imaginary. Most adults block themselves psychically by worrying, "Am I making this up? Is this real?" On the other hand, Indigo Children trust and follow their intuition without questioning its validity.

Indigo Children and the New Age of Peace

Since childhood, the angels have been giving me visions about the future. Much of the information that I receive about Indigo Children comes from the spirit world and is blended with my interviews with Indigos; and their parents, teachers, and doctors. In addition, I've found scientific studies that support many of the spiritual messages I've received.

I mention this because I realize that you may be looking for practical solutions to behavioral problems with your Indigo Children. I've received the following information about Indigos and our near future for some time:

The angels say that quantum physicists are discovering that we humans focus too much on our clocks and calendars. By focusing on time, we lock ourselves into a dense third dimension. We humans have the ability to bilocate, instantly manifest, and even levitate. Indigo Children and many spiritually aware adults know this truth, deep down. The answer is to stop focusing on time so much.

Many spiritually minded adults and children have been guided to remove their watches in recent years. As more of us do so, we'll see "miraculous" abilities reemerge in humans.

Also, many Indigo Children report that they have the ability to bend or warp time. For instance, my Indigo son, Chuck, uses time warps whenever he's late for an appointment. He says that all you have to do is think about your destination and what time you want to arrive there. "Don't look at the clock or any landmarks on your drive to your destination," Chuck counsels, "because that will slow you down by locking you into time and space. Instead, get your mind off of time completely by engaging in interesting conversation or listening to the radio. Don't speed or swerve in traffic. You don't need to. Simply keep a positive thought that you *will* arrive on time, and somehow, you'll warp time and get there promptly."

In the near future, telepathic communication will be the standard form of "talking" with one another. Indigo Children, especially the very young ones, already do this. The angels say that e-mail is the precursor to our telepathic society, because it has whetted our collective appetite for instant communication. Do you notice how frustrated you get when an e-mail takes five extra seconds to go through? The angels say that this frustration stems from our craving for mind-to-mind communication, which is telepathy. As we decide that e-mail is too slow, we'll naturally choose a faster route: telepathy.

We will become more telepathic as we start to trust our gut feelings and intuition more. Indigo Children are here to show us the way, as they're already very sure about their intuition. The Indigos won't betray their true inner feelings unless they're forced to by parents or teachers, or unless their intuition is drowned in Ritalin or other medications.

When the majority of us allow ourselves to become telepathic, a big shift in our society will occur. Why? Because no one can lie to you when you're telepathic. Just think about the institutions and systems that will be affected when lies are instantly recognizable. These systems will be forced to change their thrust and develop a foundation of integrity and honesty—or they'll crumble and be replaced.

In the 1960s, many of the first Indigos (often referred to as "hippies") were given the assignment to bring integrity to our government and other systems. But they got distracted by heavy drug usage, became disheartened by the Vietnam War and Watergate, and later got sidetracked by mainstream responsibilities.

The Indigo Children are more focused and fierce than the hippie generation, and they won't be distracted (unless we drug their Life Purpose out of them!). They *know* that the archaic educational system needs a major overhaul. They *know* that the government and legal system is corrupt. They *know* that inequities abound in health care, animal treatment, and the environment. The Indigos are here to level these systems so that we can start over. They know that there's no more time to waste.

The New Age of Peace will have us all living in cooperation and honesty with one another. In this New Age of Peace, the earth will be warm, tropical, and moist. We will live a much more natural existence, no longer craving or eating processed foods or beverages. Instead, our appetites will return to the desire for fresh fruits and vegetables, which will bountifully grow in Earth's tropical atmosphere.

Because of the warmth, clothing and shelter won't be as much of a focus for us. We will collectively let go of meaningless jobs creating meaningless objects. So, more people will work at—or near—their homes. We will be involved with work that matches our natural passions and interests. So, cars and airplanes will take a back seat to walking as the main form of transportation.

Smog, pesticides, and food additives will soon become a thing of the past. So will stress and worry. Whenever we need something, we will use the power of visualization to manifest it. Since life will be more natural, our bodies will last longer and will be more healthy.

In some of my workshops, I help audience members remember how old they contracted to be in this lifetime. Before incarnation, each of us chooses two or three ages (such as 83 and 89 years old, in my own case) when our body will shut down and our soul will return to heaven. I consistently find that Indigo Children have chosen advanced ages for their lifetime. Many of them will live several hundred years. That's because, in the New Age of Peace, our bodies won't deteriorate from stress and toxins, as they do now.

So, when Indigos don't comply and act like good little girls or boys, it's often because they're listening to their inner guidance. They've come here to usher in the New Energy of Peace, while enduring the last of the old energy of Fear. They were born during the last years of the age of Fear so that they'll be adults when the shift occurs, right around 2011. As adults, we must applaud these children for their gifts and help them channel their talents in constructive—not compliant—ways.

Purpose and a Sense of Meaning

Meaning and purpose are two concepts that are of great importance to Indigo Children. One of the reasons they rebel (through aggressiveness or forgetfulness) is because they need to understand the purpose of anything they engage in. If you'll explain *why* to an Indigo Child, they're more likely to cooperate. But if you tell them, "Because I said so, that's why," you'll be met with resistance.

When I was in school, my classmates and I questioned our math teacher one day: "What's the purpose of doing these multiplication tables?" She replied, "Someday, when you're an adult, you'll understand." We nodded compliantly and completed our work.

One of the reasons why we were able to accept her answer is that our generation, and previous ones, engaged in a process called "dissociation." We could feel in our guts a sense of discontentment with doing multiplication. All that hard work, though, would be worth it, if we only knew why we were doing it. When the teacher avoided our request for an explanation, we disconnected from our gut feelings through the rationalization of, "Well, the teacher is an authority figure, and she knows what she's doing."

But our post-Watergate Indigo Children know better than to automatically trust the integrity or knowledge of people just because they were in a position of authority. Indigos only trust people on a case-by-case basis, not because of their social or job status. You simply have to earn the trust of an Indigo.

Indigos are much healthier than we were, in this sense, because they listen to and trust their gut feelings about people. How many times have you betrayed your inner guidance that told you, "Don't get involved with this person!" and then lived to regret it? Indigo Children won't betray themselves in this way. In every situation, especially those that require effort or struggle, Indigos demand to know why they're doing something. They want to know: *What's the reason, and what's the reward?*

The angels say that we should never force ourselves to do anything. If we don't want to do something, we should instead meditate for a moment. Through this process, we can either get into a loving state of mind about a task (cooking dinner with love, or realizing that paying our bills keeps people employed, for example), or we can decide to say no to the task and mean it.

Indigo Children do this naturally by not forcing themselves to go against their natural grain. Think for a moment: Would you be more happily employed right now if you'd truly followed your heart in your career choice? And isn't this what you want for your children?

Laura Galliger, the mother of an Indigo Child named

Zachary, told me, "The only way that I can help Zachary understand why he needs to do certain things like homework is to tell him, *Well, that's the way that people on Earth do things.* That seems to make perfect sense to Zachary, because he'll then say, *Oh, okay,* and go do his homework. I feel like I'm his custodian upon this planet, helping him to know the Earthly customs. Zachary won't do something just because I tell him to, but he *will* do it if he understands that it's a customary practice on Earth."

In the New Age of Peace, people won't behave so unnaturally. With everyone following their Purpose, they won't feel so empty, angry, anxious, or depressed. So, a lot of the careers that involve quelling the human race's sense of emptiness, anger, anxiety, and depression will disappear. We won't feel compelled to eat or drink junk, buy useless widgets, or use machinery to measure time or communicate with each other. Dishonest companies, systems, and bureaucracies will either start operating out of integrity—or they'll be gone.

So, the entire job landscape will be considerably different soon after the Indigos reach adulthood. They know this, deep down, and they don't want to train for jobs in meaningless industries that are on their way out.

Instant Manifestors

People and beings who live in higher dimensions know how to instantly manifest in order to get their needs met. They focus their desire and vision on their goal, and they attract or create that objective. They've learned to discipline their minds so that they only think about what they truly want. They know that worrying creates negative results, so they don't allow themselves to do so.

Indigo Children instinctively remember their soul's ability to manifest, and they don't understand the Earthly preoccupation with training for a job, unless it's a job that dovetails with their Life Purpose. So if you talk to Indigos about "job security," they'll look at you like you're from another planet. They know that the true source of security comes from *The Source*.

In the chapters dealing with intuition, we'll discuss ways to work with Indigo Children in order to help them hone their manifestation skills. Adults can learn much from Indigos about this more natural way to meet material and spiritual needs through our God-given power of creation.

Remembering Our Life Purpose

Deep down, we all remember what our Life Purpose is. We co-created this Purpose, along with God, our angels, and guides prior to incarnation. The trouble is, we were in our Higher Self fully when we created the Purpose. Then, when we incarnated, Earth influenced us to operate from our ego-mind instead of from our Higher Self. So, we can't consciously access a lot of the material that our Higher Self knows.

Remembering your Purpose fills up the emptiness that comes from feeling like you don't matter. When you feel empty inside, you'll turn to something outside yourself to fill up that emptiness. Yet, outside objects and people never satiate an inner emptiness. Only our Life Purpose does that.

Indigo Children thrive on opportunities to help others. It gives them a sense of meaning and purpose and raises their self-esteem. As an adult, you can help reinforce the Indigos' altruistic nature by expressing heartfelt gratitude when they do something for you. A woman named Kristi related this wonderful example of how her Indigo Children—Tyler, age seven, and Sami, age four—find meaning through helping others:

> My husband, Rick, is recovering from a major illness, and he's often tearful. The other night, he was feeling very sad. He told me that he felt very disconnected spiritually. Tyler, in the meantime, was finishing an art project and presented it to his dad. It said: "The Dad Who Trusted God. One day a dad saw God. God made that dad so happy he felt so good he smiled. He told God thank you."
>
> Above the words, Tyler drew a picture of God and his dad.
>
> Both Rick and I were speechless. Tyler was most definitely God's messenger at that moment. Rick then felt more peaceful and calm.
>
> Sami is often God's messenger, too. If anyone is sad, hurt, or sick, she immediately brings that person a prized stuffed animal or doll to help them feel better. I feel so very blessed to be the mother of these two wonderfully sensitive spirits.

Remembering Your Personal Purpose

In the ultimate sense, each of us is here on Earth to remember who we are, and to be the expression of Divine Love. Yet, we also have a personal Purpose within that overarching one. Our personal Purpose is usually a characteristic or trait that we chose to work on in this lifetime.

If you discover and work on your personal Purpose, you'll heal any sense of "spinning your wheels" or feeling "stuck." There will be more of a feeling of growth, meaning, movement, and progress. These positive feelings will fill you up and remove the sense of angst that can lead to diagnoses of ADD, ADHD, depression, addiction, aggression, or anxiety.

There are a few methods that can help you and your children remember your personal Purpose:

1. Look for patterns. What kinds of situations do you and your children keep getting into in friendships, at school, or work? These patterns give clues, because our personal lessons repeat themselves until we learn them.

For instance, people who need to learn assertiveness might continually become involved with domineering friends. Once these people take a firm and consistent stance that they will no longer tolerate abuse, the domineering people will either leave or treat them with more respect. From this success, a new assertive style will work its way into their overall lives. They will stop attracting domineering people, and will take responsibility for teaching people how they want to be treated. The lesson will therefore help them achieve new heights in all areas.

Similarly, people needing to learn to focus might manifest frustrating roadblocks and distracting detours for themselves. A high school student, for example, might want to qualify for the school sports team, but she keeps getting sidetracked with other projects every time she goes to work out and practice her sport. These frustrations aren't curses; they're opportunities to learn to see the blessings within everything.

Once people recognize the lessons and take responsibility for the continual recreation of them, they no longer need the pattern any longer. After that, they'll find that life flows much more smoothly.

2. Ask your angels. Even though we humans forget what our Purpose is, our angels never forget. They are continually nudging us, through intuition or signs, toward the fulfillment of our Purpose. So, we can ask our angels to help us remember the nature of our Purpose. The easiest way is through "automatic writing." If your children are old enough to write, ask them to write a letter to their guardian angels that says, "What is my personal Life Purpose?" Then, ask your kids to write whatever impressions they receive (whether they're feeling, seeing, hearing, or thought oriented) as an answer from their angels.

If your kids are not yet able to write, you can do the same process aloud. Help your children speak to their guardian angels, and then ask your kids to tell you what they feel, see, hear, or think immediately after asking the question, "What is my personal Life Purpose?"

Or, you and your children can engage in art therapy, where they draw pictures based on the answers they receive from their guardian angels about their Life Purpose. Similarly, your kids might gather a stack of magazines and select pictures, words, or phrases that describe how they see themselves. In this way, you can see patterns that will reveal your children's personal Life Purpose. (You, of course, can utilize these methods, too.)

3. Look to your astrological sign. Before we were born, we each worked with our guides and angels to create a personal and a global Life Purpose. Once we selected our Purpose, we then chose a birth date to support our Purpose. You and your child can discover more about your personal Life Purpose by looking to your astrological sun sign. Each sun sign has a "shadow" side that refers to its negative traits. Part (or all) of your personal Purpose is to overcome, or learn from, these shadows.

Here are the personal-Purpose lessons related to each sun sign:

Aries:	Prevail over impulsive tendencies; learn to plan ahead.
Taurus:	Overcome materiality; channel stubborn tendencies into tenacity.
Gemini:	Develop your spiritual side; release the ego's self-doubts.
Cancer:	Overcome pessimism; learn to think about what you desire instead of what you're afraid of.
Leo:	Vanquish pride, and the belief that others are criticizing you.
Virgo:	Learn how to delegate, ask for help, receive good graciously, and let God answer your prayers.
Libra:	See how to make decisions and stick with them.
Scorpio:	Deal with secretive tendencies by developing more trust in others.
Sagittarius:	Learn to put your dreams into action, and complete the projects that you begin.
Capricorn:	Become more lighthearted. Develop sincerity instead of seriousness.
Aquarius:	Find out how to keep your feet on the ground while tending to your global Purpose.
Pisces:	Ascertain how to manifest abundance, and overcome the tendency to engage in needless self-sacrifice.

Remembering Your Global Purpose

Most of us have more than one global Purpose. For instance, one of your Purposes is probably to bear and raise your children. Another might involve some volunteer work that you're engaging in. And yet another might relate to the work that you do for money.

Here are some ways to remember what your Purposes are:

1. Begin with a prayer. Heaven will help you remember your Life Purpose(s), but the law of free will says that you have to ask God, the angels, ascended masters, and/or your guides (whomever you call upon for spiritual help, depending upon your spiritual or religious beliefs), before they're allowed to help you. Here are two prayers that can help:

Prayer to Remember Your Life Purpose

God and the angels, I call upon You now.
I seem to have forgotten what I came to Earth to do.
I know that I'm here to help in Your great plan of love.
Please give me clear guidance that I will easily notice
    and understand
So that I might know what steps to take today that will
    bring me closer
To remembering and fulfilling my Life Purpose.
Thank You, and amen.

Prayer to Develop the Courage to Follow
Your Life Purpose

Archangel Michael, please come to me now.
I ask you to please enter into my mind and my heart
And clear away any fears that are blocking me from

Making necessary life changes.
Please help me feel financially secure.
Please help me lose the fear of making changes.
Please help me move forward fearlessly, with full faith
    in God.
Please help me know that God supports me with the
    same energy that holds the planets in the sky.
I now give all of my worries and fears to God.
Help me to know, to believe, and to open my heart
    to Love
So that I may give Love back to God, and to all of His children.
Amen.

2. Find a cause that stirs your passion. As you read the newspaper, watch TV news, or listen to people's conversations, pay attention to your body's reactions. What news reports make you especially angry? Do any of them make you cry? Do you worry about any of these issues?

These reactions are signs that this particular cause or situation is part of your Life Purpose. Once you find a cause, it's essential that you take some action to involve yourself with it. Write a letter to your local newspaper editor, or join or start a local group. As an example, I get activated every time I hear about the mistreatment of animals who are raised for food or leather. When I was in junior high school, I channeled this passion when I started an organization to collect money to help wild mustangs, and I gave a couple of speeches at the Sierra Club. As an adult, my passion for animals inspires me to do volunteer work for animal rights organizations and to make donations to such causes.

3. Do volunteer work. Giving to others is the quickest route to gaining a sense of meaning in your life, which often encourages you to find more meaning. This can put Indigo Children on the road to looking for, and finding, their Life Purpose. If you're a parent of Indigo Children, you may want to walk them through the initial phases of volunteer work, such as helping them with phone calls and going with them the first time they volunteer.

When my Indigo sons, Chuck and Grant, were younger, we'd do volunteer work together each Christmas. For instance, we'd find the names and "wish lists" of financially troubled children, and then I'd help my sons go shopping for presents for these kids. We'd wrap and deliver the gifts together. I don't know who received more pleasure and satisfaction from the acts—my sons, myself, or the recipients of the gifts! Today, I watch with pride as Chuck and Grant generously help strangers—of their own volition.

Other examples of volunteer work include going to a convalescent home and reading a book to, or writing a letter for, the patients; helping out at your local hospice; going to a pet store and cuddling or telepathically comforting the animals; picking up litter on the street; secretly leaving a food basket or grocery store gift certificate on the porch of a needy family; donating your unwanted clothing or furniture to a domestic violence shelter; offering to baby-sit or dog-sit for free; and/or delivering a meal to a person who is unable to drive. Most newspapers and city Websites have lists of organizations that are seeking volunteers.

4. Notice your reactions to others. Sometimes when we feel jealous of others, it's because our Life Purpose is similar to that of those individuals. You can discover your Purpose by paying attention to the common thread among anyone to whom you've felt jealous of.

For instance, Brenda, one of my clients, was jealous of people who worked in artistic or creative fields. This came out one day in our counseling sessions, when Brenda admitted that she was jealous that I was a published author.

"I wish that I could make a living writing, or doing something creative!" she stated.

"What makes you think you couldn't?" I asked her. "After all, you're still a very young woman. You're obviously very creative." I pointed to the artistic way that she dressed and her colorful fingernails, each of which featured a painted flower.

"Yeah, but I could never do that for a living," Brenda said matter-of-factly.

"Why not?" I held on to the silence that hung over my question. When she obviously couldn't think of a viable answer, I asked her to remember other people whose careers she had envied.

"Well, I especially envy photojournalists," Brenda said after a few moments. When I asked her why, Brenda told me that she secretly dreamed of working for *National Geographic* magazine. She fantasized about traveling and documenting different cultures for that publication.

I helped Brenda reframe her jealousy and envy into "admiration" and "inspiration." Instead of resenting those who held jobs that she dreamed of having, Brenda learned to use these people as role models. She went on to enroll in an anthropology and photography class at the local junior college.

What I loved was that Brenda seemed energized, instead of dejected, about following her passion. While she might never work for *National Geographic*, at least she learned to empower herself by polishing her natural talents. In some way, I know that Brenda's artistic skills will benefit others. It's part of her global life Purpose.

5. Recall your childhood dreams. How *did* you, or how *do* you, answer the question: "What do you want to be when you grow up?" This will give you a real clue about your Life Purpose. My answer as a child was always, "I want to be a fairy godmother or a veterinarian." I was in touch with my Purpose of being a spiritual healer and teacher (fairy godmother) and an animal rights advocate (veterinarian).

6. Read your aura. The electrical field around our bodies contains information about our Life Purpose. The colors in this field are referred to as "auras." Many Indigo Children can see auras, and many metaphysical bookstores and psychic fairs have Kirlian cameras that take pictures of our auras, guides, and angels. Our Life Purpose shows up as a bright color that completely surrounds our body, like an eggshell. Although we have many colors in our aura, our Life-Purpose color stays constant throughout our life. Also, it completely surrounds us, rather than just showing up as a patch of color. So, you can either ask another Indigo Child to look at your aura, or have the color photographed on a Kirlian camera (also known as an "aura camera").

Here are the colors that indicate your Life Purpose, along with the four main categories related to the Life Purpose of Indigo Children:

- ***Bright Green: The Healer.*** Your Life Purpose involves helping people or animals heal their physical bodies. You might do this through conventional healing means (such as being a doctor, nurse, or veterinarian) or through alternative means (such as acupuncture, herbology, crystal healing, and so on).

- *Aqua, Turquoise, or Sea-foam Green: The Teacher/Healer.* Your Life Purpose involves teaching people, which has a healing effect upon them or others. For instance, you might teach healing methods to other healers; or teach people how to heal themselves. You might write healing books or give workshops about healing methods.

- *Light Blue: The Messenger.* This person helps the world through their communication talents. Their work could be in the form of creative pursuits that bring joy to the world, such as music, painting, photography, cooking, dance, decorating, designing, or acting. Many Messengers also go into the media, such as television, radio, newspaper, magazines, or newsletters. They also make wonderful counselors (especially if they have the gift of gab), researchers, and schoolteachers.

- *Rainbow Stripes: The Energy Worker.* Some people have bands of colors, like a rainbow, surrounding their body. Or, the bands of color may emit from the open palms of their hands. This person's Life Purpose involves hands-on healing work, or energy healing. They find true happiness and success in being a physical therapist, chiropractor, massage therapist, Reiki master, or pranic healer.

You can also discern whether you fit into these categories by answering *yes* or *no* to the following questions:

1. Do strangers tend to pour their hearts out to me and tell me their problems?
2. Do people say to me, "There's something about you that seems so familiar, like I've known you forever"?
3. Do I find myself teaching other people how to improve their lives?
4. Do I often give advice that is so wise that I wonder where those ideas came from (a "Who said that?" kind of experience)?
5. Do my friends constantly call on me for encouragement, comfort, and advice?
6. Do I love to read books or articles?
7. Do I sometimes practice speaking or singing in front of the mirror?
8. Do I seem to have a natural artistic gift?
9. Do I love to create and make things?
10. Am I constantly starting new projects that I never seem to quite complete?
11. When I put my hands on someone's shoulders, back, or stomach, do they remark how wonderful it makes them feel?
12. Do my friends and family members constantly ask me to give them massages?
13. Do I love to receive massages myself; and often massage my own hands, feet, or scalp?
14. Have I intuitively known how to "send healing

energy" to a person or animal, and felt that it had positive results?

15. Do watches tend to stop working when I wear them, or do other electrical items (lights, televisions sets, radios, cassette recorders, stereos, and so on) tend to act funny or break in my presence?

16. Do I feel like I would be, or could have been, a great doctor?

17. Do I seem to have a natural ability to know what babies want when they're crying, or what animals need when they're sick?

18. Am I fascinated with learning about new healing techniques?

19. Do I have a history of childhood illness?

20. Do I have a sense, or a calling, that I could help other people or animals live healthier and longer lives?

Interpreting your answers: Circle or underline your *yes* answers, and then notice which of the categories you had the most affirmative answers in. Read the descriptions of each Life-Purpose category in the segment called "Read Your Aura," above:

Questions 1–5: If most of your *yes* answers were in this group of questions, you're a Teacher/Healer.

Questions 6–10: If most of your *yes* answers were in this group of questions, you're a Messenger.

Questions 11–15: If most of your *yes* answers were in this group of questions, you're an Energy Worker.

Questions 16–20: If most of your *yes* answers were in this group of questions, you're a Healer.

The Importance of Discovering Your Life Purpose

At one time several years ago, I practiced traditional psychotherapy with a fair amount of success. I ran several eating-disorder units, with a waiting list of people who desired treatment for compulsive overeating, anorexia, and bulimia. I also engaged in work relating to drug addiction, alcoholism, and family and relationship issues. My work was successful enough to attract major publishing contracts for books and articles on weight, relationships, and divorce.

I appeared to be very successful. After all, I was making money and I received feedback from clients and readers stating that my work was helping them. I constantly appeared on TV and radio programs as a guest expert on various psychological topics. What more could anyone ask for?

Well, during my quiet moments, my angels would come to me to discuss this situation. They'd say, "You know, this isn't the Purpose that you contracted to fulfill. After all, look at these two indicators that you're not on the path of your Purpose: You're making money, but you don't *have* money. And you aren't finding joy in your work."

It was true. Although I was making a healthy income, I didn't have much to show for it. I was compulsively spending outside my means to compensate for my lack of Purpose.

Similarly, the sight of my byline on magazine covers or books I'd authored didn't even make my heart flutter anymore. My joy was flatlined because I wasn't working on my true Purpose.

As a psychotherapist, I had discovered that every psychological malady stems from not working on our Purpose. Depression, anxiety, dissociative disorders, addictions and compulsions, hyperactivity, learning disabilities, and low self-esteem—all result from this lack of focus. Children are no different from adults in this respect. If anything, Indigo Children hold themselves to even higher standards than most adults by insisting that every action have a reason behind it.

Some people remember, or know, what their Life Purpose is, but they're afraid to move forward—fearing success, failure, not being good enough, or ridicule. Others have no idea what their Purpose is, or they aren't sure.

When I stopped practicing traditional psychotherapy and began exclusively engaging in "Angel Therapy," I started to use spiritual methods to help people in challenging situations. I'd begin with prayers, such as the ones presented earlier. Then I'd instruct these individuals to pay attention to the Divine guidance that always comes in answer to these prayers.

Divine guidance appears as signs that we *see* (such as books that fall off of bookshelves); signs that we *hear* (such as overhearing a conversation that gives us useful information); dreams; or repetitive thoughts or feelings that urge us to do something—even if this act seems unrelated to the original prayer or intention. When we notice and follow this guidance, we are naturally led to take steps related to our Purpose. We're fully supported by God and the angels through this process, and they ensure that we receive all the time, intelligence, information, people, money, and supplies that we need to complete each step. The doors open for us each time we follow our Divine guidance.

When my clients began asking for, and following, guidance associated with their Life Purpose, miracles occurred. Their psychological maladies and behavioral problems diminished or vanished. They lost weight and began taking better care of themselves, and their relationships and finances improved.

ॐ ॐ ॐ

Your Indigo Children can use their intuition and psychic abilities to discover their Purpose. Explain to them that God often speaks to us through our gut feelings, dreams, and visions. Encourage them to trust and follow their Divine guidance.

An Indigo Child named Dawn, whom I mentioned earlier in this book, has learned to pay attention to her visions and inner guidance. Dawn says, "I definitely can see myself in the future once in a while. That's my biggest form of intuition. It's feeling a strong sense of where I should be, what feels right to pursue, and where I am in my life. Like if this doesn't feel right, I need to make a change. I've learned to follow through on these intuitive feelings."

Sometimes I'll work with a person who continually sabotages their own happiness. They'll be on the route to their Life Purpose, with everything working in their favor, then—boom! They do something to mess it up. In these cases, I always find underlying fears attendant to this situation.

Usually, people who sabotage their own happiness feel that they don't deserve happiness. They believe that they're inherently bad or defective and that they should be punished, or shouldn't receive their due. Indigo Children often feel this sense of "undeservingness" that leads to self-sabotage because of their shame about feeling different. Teachers or parents tell them that their *behavior* is bad, and unconsciously, the children hear this as, "*I* am bad." So, efforts to improve their lives fall on deaf ears, while the kids feel that they're too "bad " to receive help or gifts.

When we work on our Life Purpose, however, it's not about whether we deserve to *receive*. Our Purpose is all about giving to others. And sometimes, we need material goods to help us become better givers. For instance, a child who is going to deliver flowers to an elderly neighbor might need a wagon or a bicycle for transportation, and a vase for the flowers. That child deserves to receive those items, because they help her to give. So, we reframe the situation for her in this way: "I deserve to give. The more that I allow God, the angels, and other people to help me, the more I'm able to give to others."

You can help your Indigo Children by drawing their passions and interests out of them. Study your children, and notice what they do naturally when they're alone. Help them use this interest or skill in a way that will help others. Are they great at video games, for instance? Their happiness will come from learning to give to others via this skill. That could mean showing another child how to play the game, writing a letter to the editor of a video-game magazine with some tips for other kids, or teaching a disabled or elderly person how to access the Internet so that they can e-mail their family members.

Buy or borrow books and magazines related to your children's passions, and enroll them in classes so that they can learn more. Don't worry that your investment may be a short-term one in a pursuit that will soon be abandoned. My parents spent hundreds of dollars on guitar lessons for me, even buying me an amplifier, and acoustic and electric guitars. They only agreed to give me these items if I brought home a report card with straight *A*'s. That was all the incentive I needed, and my grades soared from *C*'s to straight *A*'s in one semester! My parents kept their agreement with me and purchased me a Fender telecaster and a Twin Reverb amp. I began playing professionally while I was still in high school.

Although I eventually gave up playing guitar (except for once or twice a month now when I "jam" with my husband, Steven, who also plays), it was never wasted time or money. Instead, guitar playing gave me a sense of confidence about being in front of an audience—which is something that is absolutely essential considering all of the public speaking I do as part of my Life Purpose.

Talk to your children about making a goal of giving to strangers or people in need a certain number of times a day. For a toddler, once a day would be plenty. Older children might enjoy looking for opportunities to give and serve twice a day. Make a game with your children when you go to grocery stores together called, "How many strangers can we help today?"

Giving doesn't have to involve money. It can mean paying a sincere compliment to someone who looks lonely or depressed, opening a door for a physically challenged person, or offering to put apples in a bag for a mother who has her hands full with her baby. These are actions that any child over the age of two can participate in. As a result, both you and your Indigo Child will find your hearts opening to joy and love through this process called "The Gift of Giving."

Channeling Your Children's Gifts

Many of your child's so-called problem behaviors are nothing more than awkwardness in utilizing their lightworker gifts. Like a baby who falls on his face when first beginning to walk, your child needs practice, encouragement, and love.

Many Indigo Children are warriors. They were sent here from heaven to help Earth rid itself of dishonesty and a lack of integrity. These kids won't succumb to apathy or social intimidation, because they have a job to do. However, their inherent warrior characteristics may be displayed as aggressiveness.

Your role, then, is to help your children channel that warrior nature into socially helpful behaviors. Teach them how to break down systems without being self-destructive. On the other hand, would you have been proud to be the mother or father of Nelson Mandela, who was willing to go to jail for his beliefs? It's a fine line that we walk, as parents of Indigo Children.

In the same way, your children's intuitive and psychic gifts make them vulnerable to feelings of fatigue, irritability, or hyperactivity. Our duty as parents is to be aware of this process, and to teach our children psychic protection and energy-healing techniques so that they can thrive and survive while fulfilling their purpose.

Our generation didn't expect us to accomplish much until we were in our 30s or 40s. The Indigo Children generation, in contrast, expects to contribute and impact society while they're still in their teens and early 20s. Understanding this difference in generational expectations helps us see why some young people delay college in favor of travel, dabbling in the arts, or getting involved in social causes.

❧❧❧ ❧❧❧

✄ *Chapter Four* ✄

Angel Therapy for Indigos

Parents often ask me, "Can I send angels to my child?" The underlying question is often, "Is it spiritually correct to do this? Will I interfere with my child's spiritual growth, inflict karmic imbalances, or offend God if I do so?" Or sometimes, the parents simply want to know *how* to send angels to help their Indigo Child.

The answer is, "Yes, you can send angels to anyone, and they will definitely benefit." After all, double-blind studies show that prayer helps people—as well as animals, plants, and even bacteria—even if they don't know that they're being prayed for. Scientific studies have shown that prayer leads to an increase in dopamine levels and also reduces anxiety, two factors that help alleviate ADHD symptoms. I've also had remarkable success (with myself and others) using prayer to eliminate cravings for stimulants such as sugar, chocolate, and caffeine, which exacerbate hyperactivity.

It doesn't matter whether you're religious, spiritual, a believer, a nonbeliever, or "naughty or nice." The angels help anyone who calls upon them. We don't have to *earn* their help. Whenever we pray, there's a measurable effect. God and the angels hear and respond to every prayer whether we recognize their responses or not.

I've had wonderful results using prayer and Angel Therapy with Indigo Children. Although my own background is Christian, I purposely keep my prayers nondenominational. After all, every religion, Eastern and Western, ancient and modern, believes in angels in some form. They may not use the exact term "angel," used in Judeo-Christian beliefs, but they believe in benevolent heavenly beings. The archangels are discussed in Jewish, Christian, and Islamic religions, but they're also definitely nondenominational.

There are a lot of Indigo Children and their parents who aren't Judeo-Christian who need and deserve the help of God and the angels. I wouldn't want to exclude even one soul just because they pray to a different ascended master than I do. I know that Jesus was all-inclusive, and this chapter on spiritual healing reflects that orientation.

You and your Indigo Children have lots of spiritual support available to you. Among the guides that you already have with you, or whom you can call to your side, are:

The archangels. Michael is the primary archangel in charge of helping Indigo Children and lightworkers remember and fulfill their Life Purpose. Michael also clears away the effects of fear from our bodies and homes, including escorting away Earthbound spirits and negative entities.

Raphael's duty is to help us heal our physical bodies, and to help healers through all aspects of their Purpose.

Archangel Gabrielle helps new parents to conceive. She

also assists people whose Life Purpose involves the arts or communication. Uriel helps us heal emotionally, allowing us to release toxic anger and unforgiveness in exchange for peacefulness.

The ascended masters. These beings once walked upon Earth as great teachers and healers, and now they help humanity from their location in the astral planes. They're associated with formal religion, but they're nondenominational and will help anyone who calls upon them, regardless of their religious or nonreligious affiliations. Ascended master Jesus is a great healer of the body, emotions, and problems. Mother Mary helps teachers, counselors, and those whose Life Purpose revolves around children.

The guardian angels. Everyone has at least two guardian angels, from birth until transition. Guardian angels are celestial beings who haven't lived as humans before, or who have walked on Earth as "incarnated angels." You can also call upon more angels for guidance, help, and protection. In addition, you can send guardian angels to others.

The nature angels. These are God's guardian angels who watch over the environment, plants, flowers, and animals. They also help people who are kind to Mother Earth and animals. Anyone whose Life Purpose involves the environment or animals usually has one or more nature angels looking over them. The nature angels are also referred to as "elementals," "fairies," and "devas."

Deceased loved ones. Our ancestors, friends, and family members who pass on often act like benevolent spirit guides. They're in heaven, but they're also able to help us. They can work on their Life Purpose through us, the living. And sometimes, our deceased loved ones are "assigned" to help us, as a Divine charge from the Creator.

Fears about Fallen Angels and Negative Entities

Many Indigo Children see frightening beings and visions in their dark bedrooms, which leads to problems with insomnia. Far removed from our generation's boogeyman fears, these psychic children really are seeing across the veil, and it isn't always pretty.

Very similar to the events in the movie *The Sixth Sense,* Indigo Children often attract Earthbound spirits who are simply looking for help. These beings don't mean to frighten your children, and they aren't out to harm anyone. They're just attracted to any human who can see them. Since your Indigo Children are born healers and helpers, the Earthbounds are even more attracted to them.

One way to deal with these spirits is to simply tell them, "You're dead, and you need to go to the Light—now!" Even better, though, is to call for powerful spiritual assistance. Teach your children to mentally say, *Archangel Michael, please come to me and escort these beings away right now.* Your children can also call on God, Jesus, or other beings related to your spiritual or religious orientation. But always make sure that Archangel Michael is among the group that's called upon. Michael's role is like that of a nightclub bouncer, and he controls who can get close to your child.

Later on, you'll read about other ways to deal with clearing your children's fears (as well as their bedrooms).

Clearing Your Indigo Children

When my son Chuck was a teenager, I often received phone calls from his teachers telling me about the trouble he'd been in that day. I dreaded these phone calls, as I'm sure most parents do.

The angels saw my distress in response to these phone calls. They came to my rescue and taught me a method to help myself, my son, and the entire situation. It involves the Archangel Michael.

More about Archangel Michael— How He Can Help You and Your Child

As I mentioned earlier, each of us has a guardian angel to watch over and help us, whether we believe it or not. The angels have managers, called "archangels." These are large and powerful angels who oversee our guardian angels.

Archangel Michael is in charge of ridding the earth of the effects of fear. He's also in charge of helping lightworkers and Indigo Children remember and fulfill their Purpose. Like all the other powerful archangels, he's nondenominational.

Michael is also able to be with everyone who calls upon him simultaneously. He doesn't have to choose between whom he wants to help. He can be with everyone simultaneously, so you needn't worry that you're "wasting" an angel's time by calling upon him.

Much of your Indigo Child's misbehavior stems from fear. For instance, your child could be ultrasensitive and may be absorbing the negative thoughts of other kids at school, or the fear of their parents' or teachers' thoughts and emotions.

As mentioned earlier, Archangel Michael is the equivalent of a "nightclub bouncer," and he clears your child's body and mind of the effects of fear. Michael also makes sure that everyone who's near your child in the spirit world should actually be there. I stated earlier that many Indigo Children have insomnia because they see the faces and eyes of Earthbound spirits, but Archangel Michael makes sure that your child's bedroom is only filled with angels of Divine light—beings who would never scare your children or keep them awake.

Archangel Michael's Vacuuming Technique

I was first introduced to this technique when I was in a deep meditation, talking with Archangel Michael. Afterwards, I called a minister friend of mine in Canada, knowing that he also worked with Archangel Michael. I said to him, "James, I have to tell you about the healing method that Archangel Michael just taught me." James interrupted and said, "First let me tell you about the method that Michael taught *me*." James and I were amazed, when we compared notes, to learn that Michael had taught us the same healing method on the very same evening!

Since that time, I've used this method on my own children and have taught it to countless adults who have successfully employed it with their own Indigo Children. It's an effective way to clear your Indigo Children of emotional toxins so that they have the opportunity to make their own decisions.

I used this method whenever Chuck was depressed or angry as a young child. Each time I used it, he immediately became "my little angel" for at least one day following. The parents to whom I've taught this method report similar success.

Anybody can call on the Archangel Michael and work with him on an equally powerful basis. You don't need special qualifications or training. Simply follow these instructions, follow your own heart, and you'll see immediate results.

The term *clearing* means escorting away the effects of fear. This can include toxic energy that your kids have absorbed from their friends, from being around drug usage, from psychic attack, or from Earthbound entities. You can work with Archangel Michael to clear your Indigo Children, their bedrooms, schools, or friends. An Indigo Child (who has natural spiritual gifts) can use this method to clear you or another Indigo. This is how it's done:

Conducting a Clearing: Asking Permission

You can either conduct the clearing when your children are with you, or "remotely" (when the children are in another location). You must decide whether you're going to ask your children's permission to conduct the clearing. Some people think that it's vital to always do so conducting a healing. You can gain this permission by mentally asking your children, *Is it all right if I conduct a spiritual healing on you with Archangel Michael?*

You will receive an impression about your children's answer. Even preverbal babies are capable of giving you a psychic answer. If you get a *yes*, then proceed. If you get a *maybe* or no, then you can have a conversation (either mentally or aloud) to assuage your children's fears.

However, other people think that it's not important to get

permission before conducting a healing. They say, "If a child is drowning in a river, I'm going to jump in whether that child gives me permission or not." You need to make your own decision about this.

After you've decided to proceed with the clearing, close your eyes. If the children are with you, ask them to also close their eyes. You may want to sit facing each other.

Visualize, in your mind's eye, one of your Indigo Children. It's important to work on one child at a time. Mentally say, "Archangel Michael, I call upon you now to clear and vacuum the effects of fear." You will then mentally see or feel a large angel appear. This is Archangel Michael. He will be accompanied by smaller angels, known as "The Band of Mercy."

Notice that Michael is holding a vacuum tube. Watch as he puts that tube in, through the top of the Indigo's head (known as the "crown chakra"). You must decide whether you want the vacuum speed to be on extra-high, high, medium, or low. You will also be directing him where to put the vacuum tube during the clearing process. Mentally direct the vacuum tube inside the Indigo's head, in their body, and around all the organs. Vacuum every part of them, all the way to the tips of their fingers and toes.

You will see or feel clumps of psychic dirt go through the vacuum tube, just like when you're vacuuming a dirty carpet. Any entities that go through the vacuum are humanely treated at the other end by The Band of Mercy, who meets and escorts entities to the Light. Keep vacuuming until no more psychic dirt goes through the tube.

As soon as the child is clear, Archangel Michael will reverse the switch so that thick, toothpaste-like white light comes out of the tube. This is a form of "caulking" material, to fill in the spaces that formerly held psychic dirt.

The vacuuming technique is one of the most powerful methods that I've ever used with Indigo Children. Even if you don't clearly see or feel anything during the process, or even if you worry, "Am I just making this up?" the results will be palpable. Most people see an immediate lifting of depression and a cessation of anger following a vacuuming session.

Vacuuming a room. You can clear your child's bedroom, schoolroom, car, or friend's room using the basic vacuuming technique. Just visualize Archangel Michael's vacuum tube suctioning the room, instead the inside of a body.

Repeating the process. Vacuum your Indigo Children every time you notice that they're depressed, angry, or acting-out. Vacuum a room every time you sense a heaviness or stuffy feeling in the room, or every time your Indigos report seeing something that scares them.

Audiotape clearing. My audio program *Chakra Clearing* (Hay House, 1997), also contains powerful clearing properties. Many people use this tape to clear rooms in their home. Simply put a cassette player in the middle of the room (use a tape player that automatically switches from Side A to Side B), and play the *Chakra Clearing* tape. Leave the room while the tape is playing. When you return, the room will be clear.

Psychic attack—a root of hyperactivity. Let's face it—kids can be really mean. They tease, hit, ridicule, and do even worse things to each other. If your children complain that they're being persecuted by other kids, chances are that they're suffering from the effects of "psychic attack."

Psychic attack occurs when someone directs an angry thought toward you. Remember the studies mentioned earlier, showing how our blood pressure and heart rates increase when someone thinks angry thoughts about us, even if we don't know they're thinking negatively? Indigo Children, who are especially sensitive to energy, are intensely prone to the effects of psychic attack.

If your Indigo Children are being psychically attacked, their nervous and cardiovascular systems are being bombarded by other people's angry thoughts. This leads to increased blood pressure and heart rates, *which may create anxiety and hyperactivity.* Your children won't know why, but all of a sudden their nervous systems will become activated. It's because of intense negative thoughts being directed at them.

If left untreated (by spiritual healing), psychic attack can become a vicious cycle, because the hyperactivity will create more situations in which your children are psychically attacked. Pretty soon you'll hear complaints from your Indigo Children to the effect of "No one likes me!"

Use this prayer to heal your children, or any other person:

Prayer to Heal the Effects of a Psychic Attack
(for another person)

"Archangel Raphael, please enter [name of person's] *body, and heal any imbalances or impurities that may have come from thoughts of anger or fear. Archangel Michael, please clear away anyone in the spirit world or the material world who is not in the highest and best good of* [name of person you're clearing]. *To the guardian angels of the person or people who psychically attacked* [name of person you're clearing], *I ask that you help to bring harmony and peace to this situation, and to replace all pain with peace. I ask that all effects of mistakes that were made, be undone in all directions of time, by and for everyone concerned. Thank you."*

Prayer to Heal the effects of a Psychic Attack
(for yourself)

You can use the above prayer on yourself if you know that someone is angry with you, or if you sense that you're being psychically attacked. Simply say "my" or "me" where you're asked to say the name of the person to be cleared.

The Pink Shield—Protecting Against Future Psychic Attack

When you find yourself in a negative situation, it's a good idea to "spiritually shield" yourself against psychic attack. For instance, if you're with someone who's complaining, judgmental, under the influence, or angry, here's a technique to protect yourself from absorbing the effects of their negativity. Or, you can use this technique to shield your

Indigo Child by picturing the other person instead of yourself in the following invocation:

> *Visualize yourself standing in a tube of pink light that surrounds you like a wall of light. This pink wall is about 12 inches away from your body and completely surrounds you. The pink light is alive, and it emanates strong, loving energy—like a sun giving off steady rays of light. The pink wall of light sends strong love inwardly to you, and also sends strong love outwardly to whomever you meet. Nothing but love can penetrate this wall of pink light that surrounds you now.*

Protecting Your Children's Physical Safety with Angels

In a recent survey of 45,000 boys and girls in grades one through eight, 70 percent reported feeling unsafe at their schools. While there have been fewer acts of violence on school campuses in recent years, the violent acts that *do* occur tend to be shocking and headline-grabbing. Whether their perception of feeling unsafe is based on reality and statistics, the truth is that our kids feel anxious and insecure about their physical safety.

I remember the first time I was confronted with my son's safety at school. Grant came home and told me that a gang of boys who spoke a different language had threatened and hit him in the locker room. Grant was enrolled in a well-regarded public high school in a safe area of town, yet I realized that I couldn't completely insulate my son from the threat of gangs and bullies.

The stress that children feel at school over grades and

popularity is now compounded by daily reminders of danger. Many schoolchildren must walk through metal detectors as they go to school, or watch armed guards or police officers patrol their campuses. These visual reminders of the threat of violence keeps children on alert. Trauma expert Bessel van der Kolk says that such conditions cause post-traumatic stress disorder (PTSD), and that people who are constantly "scanning for threats" have their nervous systems overly activated. This could lead to the symptoms of ADHD.

You can help your children feel safer and more secure by surrounding them with extra guardian angels. It has been said that when parents pray for their children, those prayers have the highest priority in heaven. Angels make wonderful baby-sitters, who will watch over your kids throughout the day. Of course, your children—like everyone else—already have guardian angels who do this, but having extra guardian angels gives your kids additional insulation against negative people and experiences. It's like putting a castle moat around your precious children!

To protect your children with angels, you can either talk to God or call on the angels directly. The results will be identical, and God won't be offended if you talk to the angels. But if you do choose to go straight to the Creator, here's a prayer you can use:

> *"God, I ask that You send protective angels to my children now. Please surround* [name of children] *with extra angels to watch over, guide, and protect them. Please let me know if I need to do anything to help with this process. Thank You, and amen."*

Another method is to visualize dozens of angels flying, standing, and circling around your children. Also visualize white light surrounding them. White light is actually the essence of angels; and is a living, breathing, intelligent entity of Divine love.

Archangel Michael is the patron saint of police officers because he protects people against physical danger. One of the ways he does so is by shifting our energy patterns so that we don't attract danger in the first place. If we do attract danger, however, Michael helps us avoid getting hurt, or to at least minimize pain and injury. Michael knows that if you think about danger, you'll attract negative people and situations to you. So, he helps you maintain a safer and more positive outlook by giving you extra doses of faith and courage.

It's a good idea to ask Archangel Michael to live with you permanently, rather than having him come and go. He's able to live with everyone who asks him to do so, simultaneously, and have unique interactions with each person. Michael doesn't believe in time and space restrictions, as humans do, so he is not limited in any way.

Simply say to him, either mentally or aloud:

"Archangel Michael, I ask that you come to the side of [name of individuals] *and live with them. Please stay by their side, and give* [name] *additional courage, faith, and protection. Please guide* [name] *very clearly in all situations so that their thoughts are aligned with Divine love. Thank you, and amen."*

If you'd like to call Archangel Michael to your own side, then say the above prayer and insert the word "me" or "my" whenever it asks you to state the name of a person.

Of course, the angels can only protect us if we listen to their guidance. For instance, the angels might send us a gut feeling that says to leave a negative situation. As such, it's a good idea to teach your Indigo Children how to recognize the signs of Divine guidance, a topic we'll look at closely in a subsequent chapter.

Etheric Cords: What They Are

If your Indigo Children are "street-corner psychologists," that is, those whom everybody tells their problems to, then their Life Purpose is probably in the Teacher/Healer category. This Purpose is described in Chapter 3.

If this is the case, your children are most likely attracting needy people into their lives. They may have friends who are chronically problem-ridden, or who pour out their hearts to them. Your children, as empathetic little lightworkers, patiently listen, and offer Divinely guided advice.

Anyone who works with other people, either professionally or by offering unpaid acts of kindness, should know about etheric cords and how to handle them. Basically, whenever a person forms a fear-based attachment to you (such as fearing that you will leave them, or believing that you are their source of their energy or happiness), a cord becomes constructed between the two of you. This cord is visible to anyone who is clairvoyant, and palpable to anyone who is intuitive.

The cords look like surgical tubing, and they act like gasoline hoses. When a needy person has formed an attachment to you, that person suctions energy from you through this etheric cord. You may not see the cord, but you can feel its effects: namely, you feel tired or sad without knowing why. Well, it's because the person at the other end of the etheric cord has just drawn on your energy, or has just sent you toxic energy through the cord.

So, anytime you've helped someone; or whenever you feel lethargic, sad, or tired, it's a good idea to "cut your cords." Teach your Indigo Child about these cords and how to cut them. It's likely that your Indigos are already psychically aware of etheric cords but just don't know that there's a term and a function associated with them.

Cutting Etheric Cords

To cut your own cords, either aloud or mentally, say:

"Archangel Michael, I call upon you now.
Please cut the cords of fear that are draining
my energy and vitality."

Then, be silent for a few moments. Be sure to breathe. You'll probably feel cords being cut or pulled out of you. You may feel air-pressure changes or other palpable signs that the cord-cutting is occurring. The people on the other end of the cord will think of you at the moment that their cord is being cut, without knowing why. You may even find that you get lots of "Just thinking about you" phone messages and e-mails from people whom you were corded to. Don't buy into faulty thinking about these people. Remember, *you* are not their source of energy or happiness. God is. The cords will grow back each time that a person forms a fear-based attachment to you. So, keep cutting your cords as needed.

To cut the etheric cords for your Indigo Children, say mentally or aloud:

> *"Archangel Michael, please cut the cords of fear
> from* [name of Indigo Children] *that are draining*
> [him/her] *of energy and vitality."*

As before, help your children remain silent and breathe deeply while Michael goes to work. Your children's mood and energy level should lift to a healthy (not hyperactive) state almost immediately.

Talking to Your Children's Guardian Angels

If you're worried about your children, or if you've had a misunderstanding with them, you can help the situation by talking with their guardian angels. You don't need special training, gifts, or other qualifications to talk to someone's angels. The only thing that you may need is practice, so you can hear the angels talking back to you.

Whether or not you're able to see or hear angels, they definitely see and hear you! Don't worry that you're in a fishbowl, being judged by heaven. God and the angels see past our mistakes and surface personality traits; they just see our talents and gifts. They love us unconditionally.

Healing a Misunderstanding

If you and your Indigo Children have had an argument, you might feel guilty. Your guilt might tempt you to give in to your children's requests, even if they're unreasonable. A better way to handle the situation begins with asking your children's guardian angels for help and intervention:

> *"Dear guardian angels of* [name], *my heart is
> heavy with hurt, anger, and guilt. I want to make sure*

that I do right by them, and I ask your help and guidance. Please talk with [name] *and help* [him/her] *to understand me better. Please help us get past our pride and egos and to express our true love to one another. I ask your help in bringing peace to this situation. Thank you, and amen."*

If You're Worried about Your Children

If you're worried about your Indigo Children, pour out your heart to their guardian angels. You can do this mentally, by speaking aloud, or by writing them a long letter. Tell the angels everything that you're thinking, including feelings that you're not so proud of. By being honest with the angels, they're better able to help you. Again, don't worry that God or the angels will judge or punish you if you tell them your honest feelings. Heaven is always aware of what we're truly feeling, but they can't help us unless we truly open our hearts to them. Talk to the angels like you would to your best friends . . . because that's what they are!

Angel Therapy for the Symptoms of ADD and ADHD

Throughout this book, I'll discuss alternative reasons behind, and solutions for, the symptoms of attention deficit disorder (ADD), and attention deficit with hyperactivity disorder (ADHD). In this chapter, we've looked at how several of the symptoms, including anxiety, depression, acting-out, lethargy, and hyperactivity, can be psychically caused and spiritually healed.

Here are some powerful prayers that may also help to reduce, control, or eliminate some of the ADD/ADHD symptoms in your Indigo Children. As you say these prayers, maintain a positive viewpoint about them. Always remind yourself, "My children are made in the image and likeness of God. Therefore, they're already healed, healthy, and well adjusted. I don't need to fix or change my children. Instead, I ask the angels to reveal the wonderful gifts and power that they naturally have. Help me to draw out my children's true strengths and talents."

If you think of your children as "broken" in any way, you'll be saying these prayers as a way to fix something. This negative viewpoint may slow the effects of the prayers. Instead, do your best to hold a vision and a feeling of your children as happy, healthy, well-adjusted people, while simultaneously saying the prayers. If you have difficulty seeing your children in a positive light, ask the angels to help you.

Say these prayers as many times as you wish (these prayers are written in the plural form; if you just have one child, substitute the singular tense).

Prayer to Heal Addictions

"Archangel Uriel, I ask that you enter my children's minds and emotions and help them lose their fear about love. I ask that all effects of mistakes made in prior relationships be undone in all directions concerned. Please help my children release any anger or unforgiveness held in their hearts. I now visualize a huge ball of bright light filling up my children. I know that my children are filled with the Light and Love of God and have no emptiness within them at all. My children are fulfilled and satisfied with the inner riches of love."

Prayer for Better Eating Habits

"Archangel Raphael, I ask that you intervene to heal my children's appetite for food. Please help them crave healthful foods and beverages. I ask that you clear away all fears or prior experiences that have created unhealthful cravings. Please give me clear guidance as to how I can help my children eat more healthfully."

Prayer to Heal Hyperactivity

"Archangel Uriel, you have the power to calm the seas and steady the earth. I know that you have the power to calm and steady my children, too. I ask that you help them feel peaceful on the inside and act peacefully on the outside. Please bring the peace of God to my children's hearts. Please help me to have patience and understanding with my children and with myself. Amen."

Prayer to Become Organized

"I now call upon the Angels of Organization. Please help my children become more focused. I ask for your guidance in reducing chaos and clutter in our lives. Please counsel my children on the value of being aware and organized, and please help them create an organizational system tailor-made to their personality. Please give me clear guidance as to how I can best help my children to become, and to stay, focused and organized. Help my children complete their projects and turn them in promptly. Thank you."

Prayer to Heal Problems with Teachers

"To the guardian angels of my children's teachers, I need your help. I ask that you help my children's teachers to have patience and understanding. Please help them release all judgments and unforgiveness toward my children. If I need to move my children to another classroom, please help this move occur swiftly and in Divine order."

Prayer to Say Before a Parent-Teacher Conference

"Dear God, I'm on my way to see my children's teachers, and I ask for Your help. Please help me be centered, peaceful, and calm. Please help me truly hear the teachers' words and underlying meaning without defensiveness or fear. Help me be cooperative and kind. And yet, let me stay strong in my knowledge that my children aren't broken, bad, or disordered. Let me be firm in my conviction against giving them medication. Please, God, help me find real solutions that will truly help my children shine, learn, grow, get along with others, and be happy. Thank You, and amen."

Prayer for the Motivation to Exercise

"Archangel Raphael, I know that you care about my children's physical health as much as I do. We both know that physical exercise provides so many benefits that would help my children. I ask that you enter my children's dreams tonight and help them find the motivation to exercise regularly. Please give my children clear guidance that they will easily understand, as to what type of exercise programs would be fun and

beneficial for them. Please motivate my children to take excellent care of themselves, and help give us any time or money that we might need to put that exercise program into motion without delay. Thank you."

Prayer for Family Peace and Happiness

"Archangel Uriel, I'm concerned that my family seems unhappy. Would you please come to our aid right away? Since this situation is affecting everyone in our household, I ask that you enter all of our hearts and clear away the residue of fear. Please undo mistakes in our thinking, and undo the effects of those mistakes. Help us see each other through the eyes of Divine love. Help us release unforgiveness and let go of blame and resentment. I ask for the intervention of the guardian angels of each and every person in this household, to bring peace and love to our home."

Prayer to Forgive Your Indigo Children

"Lord, I ask that You help me. I seem to be harboring angry feelings and thoughts toward my children. Help me release these toxins from my mind and heart. I ask that You assist me in letting go of hardened feelings. Help me to stop blaming myself, and to stop blaming my children's other parent. Instead of blame and anger, I truly desire a healing. I want the peace of God. I know that You are with me now, and I ask for Your help so that I can feel Your loving care. I now turn the situation completely over to You, trusting that the Divine mind of God already has the solution worked out. Thank You so much! "

Prayer to Heal Irritable Indigo Children

"Archangel Michael, my children seem very irritable. I know that all anger stems from fear, and I ask that you clear away the fear that is triggering this irritability. Please help my children see humor in their situation. Please help them laugh, let go, and play. Please help my children let go of blame and resentment, and replace it with compassion and patience. I ask that you clear me, as well, of any irritability that I may be projecting onto my children. And please guide me and my children if there is anything we must do or change to make the situation more peaceful and loving. Amen."

Prayer to Enhance Memory

"Dear God, I now call upon the Angels of Intelligence. I also ask for guidance from Thomas Edison, Albert Einstein, and all the other geniuses who are of God's Divine Light and Love, to come to my children now. Please help my children have access to the memory that I know that they're capable of having. Please guide my children to adopt healthful eating, sleeping, and exercise habits that will support their good memory."

Prayer for Improved Grades

"To the guardian angels of my children, I ask for your help and intervention. It seems that my children's grades do not reflect their true potential and natural intelligence. I now surrender this situation completely to God and you angels, trusting that you know what to do. Please give me clear guidance as to how I can help my children enjoy and appreciate learning, completing their homework correctly and on time, applying good study habits, and getting high test scores.

I know and trust that my children are made in the image and likeness of God, which means that they're part of the Divine mind of infinite intelligence. Please help my children enjoy learning. Amen."

Prayer for Children's Friendships

"Dear God, I ask that You help my children develop and nurture healthy friendships. Please help them attract wonderful, loving, and healthy friends. Please help my kids overcome any shyness or fears, and to be a good friend in return. Please teach my children how to be loyal, giving, and trustworthy with their friends. I now call upon the guardian angels of some wonderful new friends for my children, and ask that You bring my children and their new friends together. Thank You, and amen."

Prayer for Joint-Custody Situations

"Beloved Mother Mary, I call upon you now. I know that you help all the children on Earth, and I ask for your help with my children. Please intervene into the visitations that my children have with their other parent. Please help to ensure that my children's emotions and bodies are well taken care of during their visits. Please help me surrender to God any old anger or judgments I may have toward my children's other parent. I ask for your gentle and powerful healing energy to ensure that my children have a loving relationship with both of their parents. Amen."

Discussing Angels with Your Children

Many parents ask me about the best way to discuss the topic of angels and spirituality with their children. I find that children already know about angels from firsthand experience. Many of them saw angels, deceased loved ones, or "invisible friends" as young children, and they remember these interactions. A lot of older Indigo Children continue to have psychic experiences, but many don't know how to talk with you about it. They may fear that you'll think they're evil or crazy if they admit to their psychic experiences.

For small children, you could get out a picture book about angels and point to the picture and ask your kids, "Do you know what that is?" Allow the children to talk openly about what they feel.

For older children, you can both draw crayon pictures of angels as you casually ask them, "Have you ever seen an angel before?"

For adolescents, you might give them a tape or book about angels and see what kind of response you get. Or, you can listen to a song about angels together, watch a movie about these heavenly beings, or view the television show *Touched by an Angel* and discuss your reactions and personal experiences. Many parents bring their children and teenagers to my angel workshops so that they can learn about the angels in tandem.

If your Indigo Children sense that you're frightened by the topic of angels, they won't feel as comfortable openly discussing them with you. Discuss these fears openly with your children. You may find that they're frightened because they clairvoyantly see spirits in their bedroom or in their dreams at night. In that case, teach your kids to call upon Archangel Michael, who leads stray spirits to the light. Teach them the psychic-protection and clearing methods outlined in this chapter. And most of all, ask your children's guardian angels to help them release their fears.

Energy Work with Angry Children

When your children are angry, a red aura glows around them like fiery embers. Anger is normal, and it's unrealistic to think we can completely avoid it. But as a parent, you can diminish anger's sting with energy work. To do so, visualize yourself holding a large vase of liquid blue light. Then, mentally scan your children's energy field, looking for redness. Whenever you see or feel redness, pour some of the watery energy over it. See or feel the steam sizzle as the redness is soothed by the water.

Entering Your Children's Dreams

If you're having difficulty talking with your Indigo Children, you can have a heart-to-heart conversation with them in their dreams. There are two ways to do so:

1. Through dream interactions. Before you go to sleep, tell your unconscious mind of your intentions. Say, "Tonight, while I'm dreaming, I intend to enter [children's names] dreams and have an interaction with them. I intend that we will have a healing experience during this dream interaction."

When you wake up, you may not remember the dream, but you'll know that something happened during the night. Your children will have the same sense, and you should see evidence of a healing right away.

2. Talking in your sleep. To engage in this method, you'll have to be awake while your children are dreaming. Wait until you see their eyes moving rapidly, and then you'll know they're dreaming. This may take 20 minutes to one hour after they fall asleep. Or, set your alarm clock to wake up one hour before your children do.

Then, close your eyes and breathe deeply. Hold the firm intention of entering into your children's (or one particular child's) dreams. Next, imagine or visualize a scene of you and your children together. Visualize yourself lovingly guiding your children and having a peaceful interaction together. Give your children any messages that you'd like to deliver, such as imploring them to treat you with greater respect, drive more safely, or get their homework done. Be sure to pause and listen to your children's replies, as you would in a physical interaction.

Even if you have difficulty visualizing or staying focused, your intention of interacting with your children during dreamtime should have noticeable results. Repeat this process nightly until you see a positive change in your children's behavior.

In the next chapter, we'll look at your children's natural psychic abilities, and how these gifts can help them adjust better at home and school. We'll also discuss ways in which you can help them develop their spiritual gifts.

ॐॐॐ ॐॐॐ

❧ *Chapter Five* ❧

Intuition and Indigo Children

Indigo Children are sitting in front of the television set, changing channels with the remote control. Rapid-fire, they switch from channel to channel, instantly knowing whether it's a show they're interested in watching. They immediately "get" the gist of each show that they flip through.

These instant judgments are related to intuition. This ability to quickly grasp the essence of a situation—whether it involves meeting someone new, selecting a television program, or surfing the Internet—comes from that higher part of the Indigo Child's mind that's involved with intuition.

Many Indigo Children are "holographic learners." When someone is talking, the Indigo Child "scans" the other person and receives their information, like a computer file being downloaded. The Indigo Child must then wait for the person to stop talking about the information that has already been downloaded and digested.

Indigo Children become bored and restless in classrooms when their teachers lecture about topics that these kids already "get." Sometimes the children just know that the topic is completely irrelevant to their Life Purpose, and to the way that life will be on Earth when they reach adulthood.

Could *you* remain interested in a topic that was completely irrelevant to your life? When we were children, we listened to teachers because we were promised that their lessons would help us "someday." Indigo Children don't have the same sort of blind trust in this promise.

Some parents are home-schooling their children for this reason. Nancy Baumgarten says about her daughter, "Llael has been home-schooled since the sixth grade (she's now in the tenth) partly because of her intuitive capacities that need a more relevant curriculum with greater caring and sensitivity, and partly because she is also highly gifted academically." I've also spoken to parents who enthusiastically raved about Waldorf Schools (listed in the Resource section at the end of this book) as an alternative "holistic" approach to learning. Waldorf Schools reportedly have no incidents of ADD or ADHD among their student populations.

Impulsivity and Intuition

Impulsivity in children is also related to intuition. It's a trait considered a hallmark characteristic of the label "ADD." But what is "impulsivity"? Perhaps it's a precursor to following intuition and inner guidance. Instead of being punished or drugged for this behavior, it's a skill that needs to be fine-tuned and honed.

Sometimes impulsivity involves the sentiment: "I must have this object now!" That type of reaction usually stems from the emptiness of not knowing one's Life Purpose, and trying desperately to stop the existential pain immediately.

Hyperactivity and impulsiveness stem from the little lightworker's sense of time urgency with respect to their Life Purpose. Many adult lightworkers report having a similar feeling, like a chronic tightness in their gut. They feel a strong compulsion to "do something" to make the world a better place. It comes from an inner knowing that your Purpose is needed in the world—now. Although Indigos are still young, with small bodies, their Purposes are crucial to the world. If their Purpose is thwarted or blocked by asking them to perform meaningless tasks, they become frustrated. That is one root of their hyperactivity.

Very often, impulsivity is actually a strong instinctual response that shouldn't be stopped. Is it unhealthy to fidget when you're around a person whom you intuitively feel is dishonest? Many hyperactive and impulsive children are simply responding to overwhelming energies impeding their nervous systems.

I watched two young Indigo boys go through this recently. They were seated at a table in a restaurant with a group of people. The adults were drinking and had become loud and boisterous. Blaring music bounced off the bare stucco walls. Waiters walked quickly between the tables. The scene was definitely chaotic. The two boys reacted to all of this energy predictably. Unlike the adults, who were sedating themselves with alcohol and food, the boys chose to get up and walk around the restaurant. Their instinct to escape took over! The parents were oblivious to the boys' meanderings at first, but as soon as they noticed, they'd yell at the boys to return to the table. I wouldn't want to return to someone who was yelling at me, would you?

Then I watched in horror as the adults fed the children sugary desserts. I could tell that the children were in for an equally hectic evening. Their sensitive nervous systems would now go off the Richter scale of hyperactivity, thanks to the sugar.

Indigo Children are exquisitely sensitive to situations and people. Their intuition is hyper-alert, and they feel the impact of other people's emotions stronger than most do. Everything seems extra-intense to Indigos, so in stressful situations where they feel that adults are worried or tense, their nervous systems become overwhelmed. They deal with it through a form of exercise and movement to deflect their attention away from the stress, and even to distract the adults from their worries. It takes their mind off their fears about the adults. In addition to allowing them to escape, their movements give them time to process their thoughts and feelings. We call this coping mechanism "hyperactivity."

Sometimes Indigo Children are labeled "demanding" and "impatient." They want what they want, and they want it now. If you tell your children to wait or be patient, you're met with their temper or frustration. Intuitively, Indigo Children know that "instant manifestation" is normal. Their souls originated from high spiritual planes and planets where you could visualize whatever situation or object that you needed, and—*voilà!*—it would appear.

The Indigo Children are here on Earth to remember and teach the spiritual gifts that they intuitively know they possess. If you ask your Indigo son or daughter about manifestation, they will know exactly what you're talking about. They may not have experienced it yet, but they intuitively know and understand the principles.

The Gift of Vision

One of the reasons why Indigo Children are so good at manifesting is because they process information primarily through mental pictures. They are skilled visualizers and can easily develop a photographic memory.

Brain studies show that children labeled ADD and ADHD have higher activity and blood-flow levels in the occipital lobe, which is the area of the brain associated with sight and visions. This is especially true whenever they're concentrating on solving a problem. Indigo Children think and learn in mental pictures.

Understanding our children's thinking and learning styles helps us better communicate with them, and also helps them study and learn. Neurolinguistic programming (NLP) is a branch of hypnotherapy that looks at these learning styles. NLP practitioners have found that if you can discover what someone's learning style is (visual, auditory, or kinesthetic), you can understand them better—and be better understood by *them* as well.

People who are visually attuned notice what they see around them. When they meet someone, they notice that person's clothing, hair, height, and facial expressions first. Those who are kinesthetically minded notice the touch and smell of a new person, and how that person makes them feel. An auditorily attuned person pays attention to a new person's voice inflections, melody, vocabulary, pitch, and speaking volume.

We all have a primary way that we connect with the world, followed by a secondary and tertiary way. The next time you meet new people, notice what you pay attention to most: the way that person looks; the way they feel, smell, and make you feel; or the way they sound.

People use words to reflect whether they're visual, kinesthetic, or auditory. One of the ways you can more effectively communicate with anyone, including your Indigo Children, is to begin speaking in "their language."

For instance, with visual Indigo Children, use phrases to reflect connecting with the world visually, such as:

- "I see what you mean."
- "Please take a look at this."
- "Can you picture that?"
- "What do you see in your future?"
- "How do you view this situation?"

It's also helpful to draw pictures or write lists for your visually oriented Indigo Children. Teach them to set goals for themselves, and break them down into small steps (such as writing one page of a book report each day). Have them write these goals and steps on a chart, and help them check them off as they complete each step. You'll help them learn how to organize themselves by giving them visual tools.

By speaking your Indigo's language, you can increase the likelihood of clear communication. A former teacher of mine told the story of a visually oriented woman who was married to a kinesthetic man.

Every day, the man would come home from work and throw his work clothes on the living room carpet. He'd plop down on the sofa to read his newspaper, which he'd invariably leave strewn all over the floor. As a kinesthetic person, the man enjoyed how the experience *felt* to him, but his wife, a visual person, was horrified at how the situation of disarray *looked* to her!

She tried everything to get her husband to understand how much the pile of clothes and newspapers upset her, but nothing seemed to work. Finally, she decided to "speak his language." She said to him, "Honey, when you throw your clothes and newspapers on the floor, it's as uncomfortable to me as if I were to sprinkle potato chips all over our bed sheets."

The man squirmed with discomfort at the thought of how uncomfortable rolling around on potato chips would be. Finally, his wife had translated her visual experience into the kinesthetic language that he could understand! After that, he picked up after himself regularly.

In the same way, talk to your children in visual metaphors. Say, "Johnny, when your teacher calls me and complains about your late homework, it's as uncomfortable to me as harsh lighting [or an ugly outfit, or something else visual that fits your children's personality] would be to you."

Help Your Children Develop Their Photographic Memory

I teach classes on clairvoyance around the world, and my initial work with students involves helping them become more aware of their internal mental pictures. You can use the same process to help your children develop their visual memory. Your children will naturally develop a photographic memory in this way.

A "photographic memory" means that you can see something in your mind's eye and describe it in detail. This is very helpful in school! It's almost like cheating or having an open-book test, because you can pull up a mental image of a textbook page from your visual memory bank and read the page in your mind.

Visual children often need parental help translating their school lessons into mental pictures. For instance, if your children need to learn their spelling words, they might become frustrated if they try to learn them phonetically, because this uses auditory (or hearing) memory.

They'll do so much better if you have them focus on their natural gifts of visual memory! Ask your children to visualize the first word on their spelling list. Say, "Can you picture this word chiseled out of stone? Can you see this word carved out of wood? How about made out of brick?" The more variations that your children can see, the more likely they are to commit the word to long-term memory. Then, on the day of the test, they can simply pull the mental picture of the word into their mind's eye and "copy" each letter onto their test sheet.

You can have fun while helping your children exercise their visual mental muscles. For instance, show your kids a magazine advertisement and then cover the page. Ask your children to reproduce the advertisement in their mind's eye, and to then tell you whatever details they can mentally see. Write these details down, and then compare them to the actual ad. Be sure to enthusiastically praise your children for all the hits and near-hits that they get.

Indigo Children may seem awkward or clumsy and may be labeled as having "delayed motor skill functioning." Again, this may be your children's first incarnation on Earth. They're not accustomed to dealing with the denseness of material objects on this planet. On other planets and on the high material planes of existence, matter is more malleable. Your children may also realize that teletransportation and bilocation are capabilities of the human spirit. So, why should they bother with the clumsy and artificial means of trans-portation such as walking?

Talking and reading may also seem unnatural to Indigo Children, who intuitively know that more accurate and hon-est conversation is available through telepathy. One woman told me about her six-year-old son who had never talked. Tests for autism, deafness, and muteness showed that her son had no physical disabilities.

I tuned in to her son psychically, and his angels told me, "He *is* talking with his mother constantly. It's just that it's a psychic communication. He's so clear in his conversations that he doesn't feel the need to use his mouth to talk. That would be redundant to him."

I relayed this reading to the mother, and she immediately broke down, sobbing, "Yes, yes, it's true! I know that my son and I communicate telepathically, but I've never read about it, so I feel alone! I don't have anyone to discuss this with, so thank you for confirming this for me."

Part of the Indigo Children's remarkable intuitive abil-ities come from their visual focus. They notice every little fa-cial tic, eye movement, and shuffle of those who are talking with them. As a result, they may not make steady eye con-tact with the person with whom they're having a conversa-tion. That person may assume that the children aren't paying attention, yet the children are "hearing" the person on a very deep level.

Indigo Children are often amazing judges of character. Do you wonder about the integrity level of your new boss or boyfriend? Ask an Indigo Child. As long as you're willing to accept the truth, you'll hear it from "the mouths of babes."

The Power of Visualization

Indigo Children have powerful gifts of manifestation that are accessed through their superior visual skills. Visualization is an ancient method for creating experiences and material objects. The earliest records of visualization date back to ancient Egypt. Quantum science and consciousness studies are giving us scientific evidence of the power that human intention has in affecting matter.

So, you have a powerful manifestor living in your home! My parents knew this and capitalized upon this ability with my brother Ken and me. We were regularly called into the living room, where my parents would ask us to visualize with them. My most vivid memory is when our family needed a new car. My dad put a toy model of the type of car that they desired on top of our TV set. My parents asked us to mentally picture that car being full-sized and sitting out in our driveway. Within months, that vision came true, and we owned the car, free and clear.

I'd prefer to see parents spending time with their children learning to visualize, rather than spending time in front of the television set or reading bedtime stories. It's important to teach yourself and your children manifestation techniques with visualization. Teach your kids how to harness their spiritual gifts in this dense world. That is one of your Divine life missions that you signed up for when your soul agreed to parent an Indigo Child!

Parent-Child Visualization Projects

Help your children make a "dream board," where they cut out magazine pictures of whatever they dream of being, having, or doing. Don't limit or shame the children if they focus on material goals and choose pictures of people with great physiques, or if they cut out pictures of expensive automobiles. This is "basic manifestation," something that they have to start with. They'll soon realize that these objects can *add* to life happiness, but the objects aren't "*it.*" Then they'll turn to visualizing and manifesting more spiritual ideals.

Have your children visualize and manifest getting *A*'s and awards at school, and it will happen. As a "bedtime story," have your children visualize getting along with the kids and teachers at school, and it will happen. Teach your children to see what they *want*, not what they don't want.

Play a game with your children where you "catch" each other in negative affirmations, such as complaining or saying, "Ain't it awful" type of phrases. Give your kids a compliment or material reward each time they affirm something in a positive way.

On the morning of a school test, for instance, rally your children's optimism by having them say, "I can do it!" and "My mind is extra-alert today!" The two of you can visualize their success together on the school test, and describe your visions to each other. This will reinforce the habit of visualizing positive outcomes (for both of you!), a skill that can be applied to any situation.

Praise Your Children's Spiritual Gifts

More than anything, Indigo Children need emotional support from their parents, especially with respect to their clairvoyant psychic abilities. A parent's support can make the difference between Indigos feeling ashamed about being "different," and those who recognize the beauty of their spiritual gifts.

Jane's case is a perfect illustration. She told me:

> When my 14-year-old daughter, Leah, was 4, she told me about a conversation she'd had with God before she came into this incarnation. Leah first saw angels—huge ones—at the age of nine. It frightened her, so she shut down. She now sees what she calls "sparkies," which are sparkles of light. Leah sees them everywhere and has accepted their appearance as a very natural part of her life.
>
> At times, life is a challenge for her because she experiences it very differently from her peers. She often wonders why she's so different, and I tell her, "Your difference is the beauty of your soul. Your energy is at a different level than those around you. You vibrate at a frequency that others around you don't vibrate with at this time." Her goal in life is to help impact the world in a positive way, to connect with the world.

❦❦❦ ❧❧❧

❧ *Chapter Six* ❧

How to Heal Insomnia and Frightening Visions

Sleep may be one of the most crucial factors in your child's mood and behavior. Scientific studies and my interviews with Indigo Children show a strong correlation between the quality of sleep and whether children exhibit signs of ADHD or ADD.

Whenever I talk with Indigo Children and their parents, I consistently hear that insomnia is a problem. "I can't get my children to bed before midnight!" "My children are up all night long!" "My children see scary faces and figures in their room, and they're too afraid to fall asleep!"

Indigo Children themselves recognize the importance of a good night's sleep. An Indigo Child named Alec put it this way, "If I don't get enough sleep, I'm cranky and dull feeling."

Another Indigo Child named Elizabeth said, "I always need a lot of sleep, like eight hours. If I don't get enough sleep, I'm out of it and I'm drowsy the whole day."

Indigo Child Dawn said, "If I don't get enough sleep, I'm exhausted throughout the day. I have no energy, and I don't want to do anything. I'm just lethargic. But if I get the perfect amount of sleep, which is nine hours for me, I wake up excited about the day."

Alec, Elizabeth, and Dawn also said that getting *too much* sleep made them almost as drowsy as getting too little sleep. So, the proper balance of sleep time is essential for an Indigo Child's mood and energy levels.

Scientists have filmed the sleeping pattern of children with ADD and ADHD diagnoses, and they've found that they have more active and restless sleeping patterns than other children. Scientists in France report, "Sleep disturbances can lead to symptoms of attention-deficit hyperactivity disorder (ADHD) in children." So, not only is insomnia a *symptom* of ADHD, it can also *cause* the symptoms that lead to its diagnosis. It's rare that something is both the cause and the effect in this way. Talk about a vicious cycle!

We all know, from personal experience, how important a good night's sleep can be. Aren't you more focused and in a better mood after a restful night's sleep? Children are no different.

Sleep deprivation can also disrupt your Indigo Children's memory, reaction time, and alertness, according to John W. Shepard Jr., M.D., who directs the Mayo Clinic Sleep Disorders Center. Shepard says that tired people are also more prone to feelings of impatience, and are less interactive in relationships. So, it's crucial that your Indigo Children have a good night's sleep.

The human brain produces and stores serotonin (the important brain chemical that regulates mood and energy levels) during the dream or R.E.M. cycle of sleep. If our sleep is interrupted by anxiety, worry, or drugs, we don't get enough R.E.M. sleep. Without this type of sleep, we wake up drowsy or irritable. Many children with diminished serotonin also wet their beds, and a significant number of kids with ADHD labels are bed-wetters.

We also crave carbohydrates to self-medicate our reduced serotonin supply. A child is likely to choose a sugary, fat-filled carbohydrate in those situations, so sleep is very important in alleviating the cycle of symptoms.

Some of Ritalin's side effects, such as insomnia and rapid heartbeat, interfere with sleep. Dietary stimulants include sugar, chocolate, caffeinated sodas, artificial sweeteners, and carob gum (which is an ingredient in most nondairy "ice creams"), and they definitely interrupt sleep patterns.

Indigo Child Ryan says, "I haven't been able to sleep since I was 16, because I got put on a lot of medication from psychiatrists. I started on Prozac when I was 16. I went to a psychiatrist because I didn't seem happy; I seemed depressed. I didn't get along with people because kids are real mean in junior high. They treated me like shit. I couldn't stand being around them. So they put me on Prozac, and I've had insomnia ever since."

Aerobic exercise (running, jumping, swimming, and so on) within three hours of bedtime can also create insomnia. Ironically, though, if your children exercise in the middle of the day, they'll sleep better than if they hadn't exercised at all.

Worries about tomorrow (bullies, tests, and so on) create insomnia. Give your children, or help your children make, a "God box" for their bedroom. Any kind of box will do, including a shoe box. You can decorate it with scraps of wallpaper or pictures cut-and-pasted from magazines.

Teach your children to give their fears to God before falling asleep each night. Write the fear and worry on a scrap of paper, and put it in the box. By doing so, the children will stop obsessively thinking about the fear, and they'll be able to fall asleep.

An alternative version of the God box is to put the written fears into the freezer compartment of the refrigerator. In this way, you freeze your fears! Many people find that miracle solutions happen when they write their worries or issues on a piece of paper, and then put that paper in the freezer for a few weeks. One Indigo girl put the name of a boy who was bothering her on a paper, then froze it. Within a few days, he stopped pestering her.

Make sure your children always have pads of blank paper and pens on their bedroom nightstands so that they can transfer the worries out of their mind and onto the paper.

Insomnia Stemming from Frightening Visions

In my interviews with Indigo Children and their parents, the most surprising characteristic that I found was the huge number of Indigos who have insomnia because they see entities or other frightening visions in their bedrooms. This phenomenon is in a different category from children imagining that they see the boogie man in the closet or an alligator under the bed. The Indigos are having scary visions straight out of the movie *The Sixth Sense*.

They really are seeing monstrous faces and beings at night. Could you sleep if you knew that there were unsavory characters in your room, staring at you for God-knows-what-reason? Many Indigo Children find that their fears fall on their parents' deaf ears. Their parents say, "There are no monsters in your bedroom—now go to sleep!" So, the children lie in bed, praying that the creatures won't get them in the middle of the night. They have a fitful and restless night's sleep.

Yet, I've also met many sympathetic parents who drive many miles to come to my workshops and ask about this phenomenon. They implore me to give them answers: "How can I help my child? She's always seeing dark spirits in her bedroom!" These parents don't question the validity of their child's visions. They just want to know what to do.

I teach them how to work with Archangel Michael (as described in Chapter 4). Any child who's old enough to complain about frightening visions is old enough to learn proactive measures. Hold your child and say, "Let's call on Archangel Michael together."

Then, the two of you can say, "Archangel Michael, please come to me now and escort away any beings who aren't my angels or spirit guides. Please take them, and anything having to do with fear, to the Light right away." Spend a moment in silence, breathing, and then ask your child if he or she saw or felt anything. Most likely, both of you will have felt Archangel Michael's powerful presence. By comparing notes, you and your child help one another increase your faith.

You can also play the "Evening" side of my Chakra Clearing audiotape. It has a soothing meditation that helps people sleep (people constantly tell me that they fall asleep before the end of the tape). It also contains Archangel Michael's clearing energy.

My Indigo stepdaughter, Nicole, recalls how she had insomnia as a young girl because she'd see dark and negative visions at night. On her own, Nicole discovered that if she held a mental image of a heart with the word *love* in the middle, the visions would dissipate and she was able to go to sleep. Love does ensure that darkness cannot hurt us!

Another example of empowering your Indigo Children spiritually comes from Nancy Baumgarten, who sent me this poignant account about her daughter, Llael:

> When she was eight years old, Llael didn't feel well one evening and went to bed early. I was sitting on the floor talking on the phone when she comes running in saying, "Make them go away; there are little red devils following me!" (I don't know where she learned of devils or what they looked like supposedly, because I certainly have never told her of them, and have been particularly sensitive to the issue of suggestibility of the very young or of negative entities.)
>
> I tell her she can always remember that she can get rid of anything she doesn't want around her by saying with firm intent, "Go away; you are not permitted in my space. Only those of the Christ Light and Love may be in my presence," or something like that. She does that and then says that it's okay now.

Clearing the Room

Many people play the *Chakra Clearing* tape in rooms that they desire to clear. You can leave an audiotape playing at medium volume and walk out of the room. When you return later, you'll feel a difference in the room's energy level. It will feel warmer, happier, and clearer.

Here are some other ways to clear your Indigo Children's bedrooms so that they won't be troubled by frightening visions:

Surround your home with white light. Each night before falling asleep, visualize your entire home surrounded by white light. This will not only cleanse the energy of your home, but it will also create a barrier that keeps unwanted visitors away.

Post guardian angels at the windows and doors. Visualize, or ask for, large guardian angels to stand watch outside the doors and windows of your child's bedroom.

Paint the walls, and shampoo the carpeting. This works especially well when you suspect that your child's bedroom is inhabited by a past occupant of your home or apartment.

Cleanse with nature. Burn some dried sage (available in the wild, or at herbal and metaphysical stores), to cleanse the room's energy. For extra insurance, or if your child doesn't like the smell of sage, you can also use other elements of nature to clean the energy of their bedroom, such as:

Crystals. Place clear quartz, rose quartz, amethyst, or Sugalite crystals next to your child's bed. Hang a clear crystal in front of the bedroom windows.

Plants. Make sure that your children have live, potted plants next to their rooms. The broad-leafed plants are best for clearing purposes. During the night, the plant will absorb fear-based energy from your children's bodies, leaving them feeling more refreshed in the morning. Plus, the plant gives off oxygen, which studies are correlating with an increased ability to focus and concentrate.

Rubbing alcohol, sea water, or salt water. Place a bowl in the center of the room, and fill it with either rubbing alcohol, sea water, or water that you've poured sea salt into. The liquid absorbs negativity from the air, and also cleanses your children's chakras.

Feng Shui Methods to Help with Insomnia

Your children may be suffering needlessly from insomnia, because the layout or "Feng Shui" of their bedrooms triggers anxiety, says Terah Kathryn Collins, author of three books on Feng Shui, including *The Western Guide to Feng Shui—Room by Room* (Hay House, 1999). Feng Shui is the study of how to arrange our environment to enhance our lives, and it teaches us about the importance of the placement of items in our homes.

In an interview I conducted with her, Collins told me:

> Before parents put their children on Ritalin, they should first change the children's linens. Most children's bed sheets, bedspreads, and room decorations in general are much too stimulating. They are made with the brightest primary colors: red, yellow, blue. The images filling many children's bedrooms are stimulating pictures of superheroes, fantasy characters, or automobiles flying, falling, driving, and running around the room.
>
> I ask parents, "Would you sleep in this room?" Usually, they wouldn't want to sleep in their own children's rooms, because the color scheme and decorations aren't relaxing. Instead of bright, primary colors, we need to decorate our children's bedrooms in what I call "Teddy Bear colors," which relax the children and help him or her to sleep. Teddy Bear colors include a wide range of skin toned and deep rich colors, such as cocoa brown, peach, muted yellow, and pale lavender.

Also, place mirrors away from your child's bed, as they are also very stimulating and tend to keep the bedroom "awake" all night long. Mirrors can also frighten children, because they see images that they imagine to be ghosts or monsters reflected in the mirror.

Having dozens of stuffed animals staring at your children, in his or her bedroom, can also be too much of a good thing. The children have likely named all of the stuffed animals, so there are soul fragment energies coming back at the children from the toys, just as if they were alive. And finally, please make sure that the pictures on the walls promote calmness, with no frightening or threatening images such as witches or gremlins. Children respond very well to having photographs of parents, grandparents, and other loving adults in their bedroom, as they help the children feel safe and protected through the night.

The point is to encourage calmness and rest in your children's bedrooms. If you can have a separate area of the house for your children's computer and homework, so much the better. It's best to design the bedroom to be a sacred space devoted just to relaxing, resting, and sleeping.

Indigo Children and the Invisible Realm

Sensitive Indigo Children aren't just affected by the physical properties of their bedrooms; they're also influenced by the invisible nontangibles in their rooms. Music, lighting, and scent can make a big difference in your children's sleeping patterns, moods, and energy levels.

Music. From the time of Pythagorus in ancient Greece, human beings have used music as a healing agent. You may worry that your children's choice in music is exacerbating depression, hostility, or anxiety. In those cases, I've always encouraged parents to sit with the children and essentially say,

"Can I listen to this song with you?" And then gently ask, after the song is over, "What does this song mean to you? I didn't understand the lyrics; what are they saying?"

I've found that I connect with my two Indigo sons and two Indigo stepdaughters by keeping abreast of current musical hits. I watch music videos on VH1 (a television station devoted to current music), and listen to popular radio stations. And you know what? I really like most of what I hear and see. I swap CDs with my sons and stepdaughters, and we sing together.

But there's also some negative energy in certain songs. If my children started obsessively listening to dark-themed music, I'd pay close attention to their demeanor and dress. If they started dressing in all black, or if my stepdaughters started wearing black lipstick, or if their body language was slumped over, with their eyes cast downward, I'd talk to them. Those are all signs of depression.

Depression among children is a serious epidemic. More than 2.5 million children are currently taking antidepressants. Untreated and unrecognized depression all too frequently leads to suicide, which is one of the leading causes of death among young people. In addition, researchers say that depression can precipitate inattention and impulsivity, symptoms of ADHD.

If you're concerned about your children being depressed, I'd begin with prayers. For instance,

> *"Dear God, I'm afraid that my children are depressed. Please help to lift my fear so I can clearly hear Your guidance as to how to best help them. Please God, Holy Spirit, Jesus, and Archangels Michael, Raphael, and Uriel, intervene into my children's*

hearts. Help them release any darkness that's robbing them of joy and vitality. Please help my children to be joyful and peaceful. Thank You, and amen."

If you sense any serious suicidal behavior, or if your children make remarks about dying, it's time to call for professional help. Even licensed psychologists call for help if their own children become suicidal, because we're often unable to effectively help a clinically depressed relative or friend.

In the absence of suicidal ideation and dark music, however, music in general has been shown to be helpful in meditation. When life is stressful, scientists have observed that music slows our heart rate and reduces anxious behavior. Studies also show that music helps us open up to our psychic abilities. In addition, music has been shown to help reduce the perception of exertion during exercise workouts.

Music has also improved arithmetic performance among children labeled ADHD in one study conducted at Schneider Children's Hospital in New York. The researchers concluded that music might provide extra stimulation that energizes children and inspires them to attain a higher level of performance. So, if your Indigo Children insist on listening to fast-paced music while completing their homework, they may intuitively realize the need for the boost that music provides.

"Drumming circles" are a musical option that you may enjoy engaging in with your Indigo Children. Basically, a drumming circle means that everyone sits in a circle and beats on a drum or shakes a rattle. Each member of the group plays their own rhythm, but eventually, everyone's rhythms become synchronized. A recent study has shown that drumming circles increase the immune system response and can create more robust health in the face of stress.

Besides that, it's fun! My husband, Steven, introduced me to drumming circles as a result of his studies of shamanism and the spirituality practices of indigenous cultures. The first time I tried it, I was a little intimidated (could I play well enough?), but after a few minutes, I lost my inhibitions and really started having a good time. We've often conducted drumming circles with our children and friends, and everyone enjoys the unity that it brings about.

You and your Indigo Children can drum together, with a group, or as a small band of two or three. Anything can serve as a drum: a can of oatmeal, a bottle of vitamins that you shake, or a baking pan. Most music stores sell native drums, or you might enjoy making your own.

Lighting. The lighting in your kids' bedrooms also affects their mood and energy level. If your kids study in their room, they need adequate lighting near their desk. A three-way light bulb that adjusts to different levels should provide adequate lighting.

It's essential that your children be shielded from household and street lights when they're trying to sleep. The angels have taught me that even a soft light in the bedroom can create low levels of interference with deep sleep. If your children insist on a night light, keep it as dim as possible, and out of the line of vision with their head as they sleep. Close your children's bedroom door to shut out lighting and sound interference from the general household. Make sure that your children's curtains or blinds adequately shut out street lights and sounds.

Always remember how sensitive your Indigo Children are to the environment, which includes lighting. In fact, lighting can affect your children's ability to concentrate and focus. Daniel P. Reid, author of *The Tao of Health, Sex, and Longevity*, believes that fluorescent lighting and lack of sunlight (what he terms "chronic ultraviolet deprivation") is partially responsible for hyperactivity.

Reid writes:

> When ordinary fluorescent lights were replaced with full-spectrum lighting in typical classrooms where severe behavior abnormalities had been observed, violence and hyper-tension disappeared within weeks of the change in lighting, and former "problem children" turned out to be model students. This positive result was observed in every classroom tested.

Reid says that we need daily doses of sunlight, unfiltered by glass windows or sunglasses. In this way, we're exposed to full-spectrum light. Sunlight triggers the pituitary and pineal glands. Since the Indigo Child's third eye (the site of the pineal gland) is more open than most, they need more full-spectrum lighting than most. Seasonal Affective Disorder, a form of depression, is a factor when people are deprived of full-spectrum lighting.

Along the same lines, Jeffrey Freed, M.A.T., author of *Right-Brained Children in a Left-Brained World,* says that many ADD children are extremely sensitive to lighting conditions. He writes: "I've noticed that many of these students have trouble focusing in school because of the almost painful glare of the lighting." Freed says that harsh classroom lights create reflections on the pages of children's reading material, creating additional distractions that make it difficult to concentrate. As a result, Freed writes, "The child reports a jumbling of the words, and the resulting frustration leads to poor reading."

Daniel Reid agrees with Freed, and he also contends that the flickering lights of television sets aggravate children and promote hyperactivity, which could also lead to insomnia. Reid cites a study in which rats were placed next to a color television set (for six hours daily) that was covered with heavy black paper so that only the invisible rays came through. The rats became hyperactive and extremely aggressive, symptoms that lasted for at least seven days. Reid contends that "the damage from television rays is caused not by the visible spectrum, but by invisible radiation contained within it."

Smells. You've probably heard of "aromatherapy," the alternative health practice of using essential oils and flower essences to positively impact health, mood, and energy levels. Well, science is corroborating the powerful effects of smell and aromatherapy. New studies show, for instance, that the scent of lavender has measurable sedative and relaxing effects.

To help your children relax and sleep better, make or buy a "sleep pillow." Usually, these are made of silk cloth, stuffed with flaxseed, and scented with lavender oil. You can purchase these eye pillows (small, long pillows) or "dream pillows" at health-food stores, yoga studios, and metaphysical centers.

However, you can also sprinkle lavender oil (which you can purchase at any health-food store) on your children's pillowcases and sheets and gain similar results. If you can find the oil of valerian root, this has also been found to be an effective sleep agent.

My Indigo Children also enjoy the smell of "Nag Champa" incense, reputed to be formulated in India for the spiritual avatar (master) Sai Baba. It smells wonderful and has a relaxing quality to it.

Indigo Children are extremely sensitive to smell. If your Indigo Children complain that they don't like the smell of something, believe them! They're probably more aware of scents than we adults are, and arguing with the children, or thinking they are histrionic, isn't effective. Instead, help your children set up their bedrooms and other environments with pleasant smells based on natural fragrance (since artificial fragrances tend to worsen the symptoms of ADHD).

Take your Indigo Children to a health-food store's essential oil counter, and allow them to purchase their favorite scents. Not only will you bond with your kids during this experience, you'll also earn their gratitude because you're acknolwedging how sensitive they truly are.

Touch. Your Indigo Children's sensitivities also make them aware of the comfort level of furniture, linens, and clothing. You might feel frustrated that your Indigos won't wear half their wardrobe because they complain that it scratches or binds them, but these are very real problems in the material world they live in. Most Indigo Children don't like synthetic fabric, since they tend to have an aversion to anything unnatural. They do better wearing 100 percent cotton, especially the organic variety that lacks the perfumes, pesticides, and other chemicals to which Indigo Children are frequently allergic.

As mentioned previously, Terah Kathryn Collins, the Feng Shui expert, noted that most children's linens are much too brightly colored, and that these hues are so stimulating that they actually keep children awake! I remember, as a child, that I had sheets featuring characters from the movie

The Wizard of Oz. I'd contort my body so that I wouldn't touch the Wicked Witch, whose picture was scattered across my sheets and pillowcases.

I've also noticed that children's sheet sets tend to be made from coarse, rough fabric. Instead of spending extra money to decorate your Indigo's bedroom in images of the latest cartoon or movie, why not invest in comfortable sheets? A high-thread-count cotton sheet could be the best gift you ever give to your kids.

Also make sure that your Indigo Children's beds are long enough to accommodate their growing bodies. Test the pillows: Are they comfortable? How about the blankets? And most important: Ask your children for feedback about their degree of comfort in bed. Press them for details. When I did this with my son, Grant, I discovered that he preferred to sleep on velour blankets rather than sheets. I took him shopping, and we had a meaningful bonding experience while we touch-tested blankets until we found just the right degree of softness. His sleep quality improved dramatically after that.

Electromagnetic Frequencies (EMFs). Indigo Children, as I've emphasized in this book, are exquisitely sensitive, emotionally and physically. They may not realize why they're hyperactive, but they're unconsciously aware of stimulants and irritants in the environment that irritate them. They also have an interactive effect with battery-operated and electrically charged items. (A lot of Indigo Children find that watches stop working when they wear them, and that electrical items break or don't function in their presence.)

One of the irritants found in the bedrooms of Indigos comes from electromagnetic frequencies, often referred to as

EMFs. Several studies have correlated EMFs with serious health conditions. Your Indigo Children may experience central nervous system "arousal" because electrical appliances are near their beds.

It's essential that everything that's electrically charged or battery operated be situated far from the child's bed. So, make sure that the television set, electric clock, plug-in telephone or answering machine, and computer are at least four or five feet from the bed. Don't keep any electrical appliances (clocks, phones, and so on) on your child's nightstand. It will interrupt their sleep, guaranteed. And, as mentioned previously, interrupted sleep relates to an increase in ADHD symptoms.

Night, Night

When you teach your children spiritual clearing and protection methods, you're giving them a magnificent gift. First, you reassure them that you truly understand them. Second, you show your love for them; and third, you guide your children to begin working with their angels, which helps them throughout their childhood, adolescence, and adulthood.

Indigo Child Dawn shares how her psychic visions have helped her feel safe and protected:

> I have a lot of dreams that are premonitions about what will happen in the next few days. For instance, when my boyfriend cheated on me, I didn't know about it for a month. But during that month, I had recurring dreams that my boyfriend was cheating on me. I didn't know where it was coming from because I felt so happy with him. And then I found out the truth and I thought, *Whoa, I should have listened to that.*
>
> I've had other mystical experiences as well. For instance, I had never met my great-grandpa, but everyone in my

family praised him for being a giving and kind spirit. When I was seven years old, I was sitting in my hallway. Suddenly, I saw a green hazy figure, and I wasn't scared at all for some reason. I briefly saw this glimpse of his face, and I knew that it was my great-grandpa. He was letting me know that he was there and that he was a guardian. I definitely now feel a sense of safety or security. I know that there are angels around me at all times. If not one, many. I feel like I am very highly protected in this world because I have never had anything really bad happen to me. I've never broken a bone in my body; I've never been in a car accident. Knock on wood, but I don't feel like I have to.

When Indigo Children know that they're being watched over by God, the angels, and by their parents, they can be assured that all is well.

❧❧❧ ☙☙☙

❧ *Chapter Seven* ❧

Exercise: Shifting Brain Chemistry and Behavior Naturally

What if the world of science discovered a pill that could instantly alleviate depression and anxiety, and also help a person lose weight, live longer, and feel happier? And what if this pill was freely available to everyone, without a doctor's prescription and at a relatively low cost? All the newspapers would herald this remarkable discovery. People would clamor to buy the pill!

Well, such a cure-all does exist, and its effectiveness is backed up by countless scientific studies (many of them are listed in the bibliography of this book). It's called "exercise." Studies show that aerobic exercise in particular—running, jogging, stair climbing, swimming, bicycling, and brisk walking—increases the production of the brain chemical *serotonin* and other feel-good neurotransmitters.

Several ADD and ADHD experts have stated, "If children would jog once or twice a day, we could virtually eliminate the need for Ritalin prescriptions." Yet, because no pharmaceutical company profits from exercising, physical fitness isn't pushed as vehemently as stimulants.

According to the Centers for Disease Control and Prevention, nearly half of American youths aged 12 to 21 years are not vigorously active on a regular basis. Only 19 percent of all high school students are physically active for 20 minutes or more, five days a week, in physical education classes. About 14 percent of young people report engaging in no recent physical activity. Inactivity is more common among females (14 percent) than males (7 percent), and more prevalent among African American females (21 percent) than Caucasian females (12 percent). Participation in all types of physical activity declines strikingly as age increases.

Daily enrollment in physical education classes dropped from 42 percent to 25 percent among high school students between 1991 and 1995. Yet, well-designed school-based interventions directed at increasing activity in physical education classes have been shown to be effective. Social support from family and friends has been consistently and positively related to regular physical activity.

I've recommended exercise for my eating-disordered and depressed clients for years, based on my personal and clinical experiences. After all, many eating disorders are triggered by strong emotions and also by food cravings that are regulated by serotonin production. Since exercise helps on both counts, those who work out regularly are more apt to heal from eating disorders.

I run six to seven times a week, work out with weights three times a week, and practice yoga regularly. On a typical run, I'll start out feeling sluggish and not really "in the mood."

During the first five to ten minutes, my feet and body feel heavy and unresponsive. But somewhere along the run, I'll feel my breath deepen so that my entire lungs take in air. My body relaxes, and my stride lengthens. That's when the magic happens, and then it feels like I'm gliding effortlessly across air.

After the run, I feel exuberant yet relaxed. Any worries or cares I had before the run seem incidental. I feel like everything is under control, or is surrendered to God. At these times, I often wonder, *How can anyone feel good unless they're exercising regularly?*

Getting Motivated to Exercise

I'm realistic. I know that most people consider exercise to be boring, painful, and time-consuming. I often feel the same way! Federal figures show that 60 percent of us aren't exercising enough. Other surveys show that the majority of us consider health and an attractive figure to be an important goal, yet we aren't willing to work toward that aim.

I believe that these feelings stem from a principle of human behavior given credence in psychological studies: Presented with the choice of completing two tasks—one important but difficult, and the other unimportant but easier—most of us will opt to complete the latter one first. Then, we never get around to completing the priority that may require more effort. So, countless books and masters' theses go unwritten, garages remain disorganized, and miles go "unrun" because we have other things competing for our time.

A major reason why we procrastinate completing important tasks is because our ego (or lower self) is afraid for us to work on our Life Purpose. Anytime we work on something that could improve our lives, or the lives of others, the ego protests. It engages in "delay tactics," which are methods that waste time so that we won't remember who we are and why we came to Earth.

The circular dilemma for all of us is that, if we're not working on our Life Purpose, happiness is nearly impossible. We feel empty and guilty. The inner realization that we're supposed to be doing something else that's more meaningful and important gnaws at us whenever we waste time.

This is not to say that relaxing with friends or family is a waste of time. In fact, whenever we engage in a love-based activity, it *is* part of our Life Purpose. The ego draws us to fear-based actions such as addictions and obsessions. These actions lower our energy and self-esteem.

Why Exercise Is Essential for Indigo Children

Indigo Children realize when they don't feel well physically or emotionally. They know that something is "off." They try eating, drinking, smoking, shopping, romance, Internet surfing, playing video games, and compulsive television watching. These activities initially improve their moods and alter their brain chemistry. Yet, the highs are always followed by crashing lows. So, the Indigos search for other ways to find contentment.

Noncompetitive exercise of the aerobic variety is one of the only variables that truly allows Indigo Children to naturally control their moods. Diet, food, and sleep all play essential roles in reducing ADD and ADHD symptoms, of course, yet exercise is key because if children are forced to stop eating certain foods but still crave them, these kids will find a way to obtain and eat those foods. Like drug addicts trying to medicate themselves, clever Indigo Children who crave sugar . . . will get sugar. If your children have eaten junk food all their lives, it's unrealistic to think that you'll be able to step in and abruptly alter their eating patterns.

Yet, through a combination of spiritual healing (using angel therapy and prayers) and helping your children find the right exercise program, you can realistically help your children eliminate their junk-food cravings. A person who exercises regularly begins craving healthier foods and reduces their desire for unhealthful items. The result will be that your children won't be fighting their appetite, and you won't be engaged in a power struggle over what they eat.

In addition, studies show that exercise increases the quality of a person's sleep and reduces insomnia. The only exception is when we exercise within three hours of our sleeping time. Then, our heart rate and body temperature rise too much for us to easily fall asleep.

Making Exercise Fun

Most likely, your children associate exercise with their physical education (P.E.) classes at school. Since Indigo Children tend to be shy, sensitive, or even socially phobic, P.E. is often an excruciating experience. Coaches force them to run, and kids tease or bully them. No wonder they relate exercising to emotional pain!

To help your kids overcome these feelings, choose a fun workout such as renting a bicycle-built-for-two, rowing boats together, or going on a family hike. Suggest that your children listen to music while exercising. At least two major studies have found that doing so reduces the feeling of drudgery associated with the activity and makes time seem to pass faster.

I normally run outside, which is a great idea for Indigos, since studies show that sunshine and fresh air stimulate production of the feel-good brain chemicals, especially serotonin. Since cardiovascular exercise already promotes serotonin, exercising outside is like getting a double dosage. However, during inclement weather, I'll run on a treadmill. During those times, I love to watch music videos to entertain and inspire me.

Here are some additional ways to motivate your children to adopt an exercise program:

- Buy your kids a subscription to an inspirational monthly magazine about exercise, such as *Runner's World, Shape, Fitness, Men's Fitness,* or *Yoga Journal.*

- Invest in a good pair of shoes that are appropriate for your children's exercise choice, as well as heavy running socks.

- Seek out sporting-goods stores that sell used athletic equipment such as bicycles and treadmills at bargain prices.

- Attend (or watch on television) track meets, basketball games, or tennis matches with your kids to stimulate their interest in sports.

- Offer your children incentives for exercising, such as a small amount of money or a new CD from the music store. It's important that you compliment them on their efforts, too.

- If your Indigo Child is a teenager or older, invest in a family membership to a gym or health club. You'll get to spend more time together, and also have the opportunity to work out in close proximity to each other.

- Probably the most valuable gift you can offer your children is to exercise yourself. Whether you know it or not, your children watch and react to whatever you do. Sometimes your children counterreact (do the opposite), and other times they mimic you. My parents are avid exercisers, and they definitely inspired me to adopt a healthful lifestyle. Find out what time of day your energy levels are at their highest, and work out during that time.

Eastern Forms of Exercise

Yoga, tai chi, and other Eastern forms of exercise can be especially helpful for Indigo Children as they learn to focus and concentrate. They also teach Indigos how to center themselves so that when they become upset, they have self-regulating tools to use. Through the use of breath and mindful movement, Indigo Children learn how to be masters of their thoughts and bodies.

Many yoga centers offer classes for children and young adults. I've found that yoga helps us meditate and lose negative thought patterns. It's especially useful for people who complain that they have difficulty meditating because their mind is too busy or noisy, or because they fall asleep during meditation.

When my sons were young, I enrolled them in a tai chi

class. Not only did they love it, but their grades immediately soared upward!

If you're worried whether your children will have the motivation or patience to begin, and stick with, an exercise program, it's a good idea to ask for heaven's help. Here's a prayer:

> *"Dear God and guardian angels of my children, please help my kids find an exercise program that will be fun and meaningful for them. Please guide them so that they clearly understand what kind of workout program would best be suited to their personality and our lifestyle. Help me be motivational, but not controlling; inspiring, but not interfering, with my children's exercise program. Thank you so much, and amen."*

ᴗ⁴ *Chapter Eight* ᴣᴗ

Natural Children in an
Unnatural World

Every few years, a movie will come out about a "feral"
person—someone who was raised in the wild—trying to
merge into our modern society. For example, the movie *Cast
Away* starred Tom Hanks as a man who had difficulty re-
entering the world after being stranded for years on a desert
island. A similar theme is found in movies where a person
from the past time-travels forward into modern times.

These films usually show how awkward it is for a person whose background is based on simplicity to deal with our
complex, technological society. In a way, Indigo Children are
dealing with similar challenges. Yes, they've adapted to the
technology of computers, but for the most part, Indigos don't
understand a lot about worldly affairs.

Connecting with Nature

Our souls hunger for a connection with the great outdoors.

So often we spend our lives inside, in buildings with fluorescent lighting and circulated air conditioning. Days go by without us touching grass or trees. Studies show that the human body needs sunlight and fresh air. Not only does our optimum health depend upon our being outside, but so does our ability to concentrate, focus, and sleep, according to dozens of scientific studies.

Since exercise is essential to the well-being of Indigo Children, it's best that they exercise outside. Running on a treadmill is vastly different from running outdoors. For one thing, exercising outdoors uses a wider variety of muscles. And since sunlight, fresh air, and exercise all produce serotonin, we get the biggest boost of this feel-good brain chemical when we work out in nature.

Indigo Children who have a Life Purpose involved with helping the environment especially need to connect with Mother Nature. They may need alone times where they can walk and think in the wilderness. If you live near trails where your Indigo Children can hike, please encourage them to do so! This is the true church, temple, and classroom where your Indigos learn and pray. If you live in a city without natural surroundings, then please consider sending your Indigos to visit your relatives who have a farm, or to a wilderness camp on a regular basis.

Gabrielle Zale, a youth art, music, and drama therapist, recalls how some of her students have been impacted by being in nature:

> The girls at my center created a beautiful painting as a group project. Each girl's group painting theme was always the same: "peace." One group created a painting that was a winter scene in which they used the peaceful colors of blue and lavender, white snow, a small river running, and

a colorful tree. Each girl contributed to the whole of the painting using a flowing focus. The painting was hung in the reception room.

I asked the girls one day: "If you could create a place here in this building that would be your very own, what would you create?" These were the words they used: "A peaceful place," "A place to kick back," "A neutral place," and "A quiet place to draw or paint." After hearing this, we went to the mountains and gathered pine cones, wood pieces, and rocks. I found that these children were very natural and thrived on Mother Earth and Native American energy.

Ultrasensitive Indigo Children

You may feel frustrated because your Indigo Children are often impossible to live with. It may seem that everything upsets them!

But look at it from the Indigos' point of view: They feel things so much that it's sometimes painful. They become overwhelmed by the emotions they pick up from other people, so they may avoid intimate settings that promote one-on-one conversations. For example, they may clam up at the counselor's office because they intuitively know that this person has a personality disorder. They absorb other people's fear thought-forms, and their systems become clogged. If you feel that this might be the case with your kids, be sure to teach them the vacuuming technique described in Chapter 4.

Indigo Children tend to be very picky about the comfort of their clothes and shoes. My son, Chuck, would constantly take his clothes off when he was small. He'd complain about how uncomfortable "normal" clothes were, and he'd live in sweat pants and sweatshirts. Even then, he'd stretch out the collar of his sweatshirt so that it fit loosely around his neck.

In a similar way, some Indigo Children complain that clothing labels on the inside neck area of their shirts cause them irritation or itching.

A lot of Indigo Children develop allergies. Synthetic fabrics and pesticides on cotton can cause them to itch, develop hives and rashes, get asthma, and become anxious. If you suspect this might be the case with your kids, try clothing them in organic cotton. The skin sensitivity of Indigo Children can also lead to allergic reactions to laundry detergents (except for the type sold in health-food stores).

Unnatural Additives

Since Indigo Children are so sensitive, and because they have difficulties adjusting to synthetic and unnatural chemicals, you may need to adjust your household cleaning agents as a way of helping your kids.

Children are more prone to the negative effects of environmental toxins than adults are, according to the National Academy of Sciences and the American Academy of Pediatrics. Both organizations say that toxic chemicals can trigger, or worsen, behavior problems.

In addition, food dyes make a child's ADHD symptoms (such as hyperactivity, impulsivity, and inattentiveness) worse, according to 17 double-blind scientific studies. This research also shows that when food dyes and other food additives are removed from the diet, the ADHD symptoms diminish or disappear.

As mentioned earlier, many Indigos are clairsentient, and this gift also encompasses the "olfactory sense," or the ability to smell. This is an instinctual gift that Mother Nature provided for us so that we could avoid rotten food and detect danger (such as fires). As we depended less upon our instincts for safety and more upon technology and government authorities, we lost touch with our sense of smell.

We were able to handle the scent of heavy perfumes in our cologne and cleaning products, and could even decide that we "liked" the scents. Indigo Children, with their instincts intact and sense of smell in its natural state, don't have a tolerance for artificial smells. They need fragrance-free cleaning products, or those that are organically produced with natural flower essences.

Barb, who has taught elementary school for 19 years, says:

> Children have changed drastically since the beginning of my career. When I started teaching, I rarely heard about the drug Ritalin. Now we have epidemic numbers of children taking this drug so they can cope with the school system or, should I say, so the school system can cope with them!
>
> With increased class sizes and new curriculum demands, these children are forced into a stressful situation that they don't know how to cope with. Their teachers don't know how to cope with them either.
>
> Through their behavior, these children are clearly telling us that they need fresh air, exercise, healthy food, playtime instead of television time, attention from their parents, and less stress. I have never found a child who misbehaves without a reason.
>
> We, as the adults in their lives, have much to learn from these Indigo Children who have wisdom beyond their years . . . if only we choose to listen to them.

Detoxing Our Bodies

The angels encourage us to detoxify our bodies, and you and your Indigo Children may even find that you've received some intuitive urgings to make changes in your diet and lifestyle. These are very real messages that you're receiving from your guardian angels. You're not imagining them.

The angels ask us to stop consuming toxins in the things we eat, drink, and use on our bodies. Toxins pull down our energy levels and make us feel sluggish. They also block our ability to clearly receive messages from heaven and interfere with our spiritual growth.

The main toxins that the angels ask us to avoid are:

- **Meats, fowl, and fish contaminated with hormones and pesticides.** Since virtually all animal flesh and by-products (milk, eggs, cheese, and so on) have residues of hormones and pesticides, you may consider adopting a vegetarian lifestyle or a near-vegetarian lifestyle (where you eliminate animal products once or twice a week). If you feel you must consume animal products, purchase "organic" dairy products (such as Horizon brand milk), and free-range chickens, hormone-free meat, and eggs from free-range chickens. These products are available at health-food stores, as are wonderful meat and fowl substitutes such as seitan, glutan, tempah, and baked tofu. Vegetarianism has come a long, long way in the past five years. If you haven't tried vegetarian meals in a while, give them another try—they're now delicious and difficult to distinguish from meat products.

- **Pesticides on fruits and vegetables.** Try to eat an all-organic diet. Ask your grocer to carry organic produce, or find a health-food store or fruit stand in your area that sells organic fruits and vegetables. However, according to Vimala Rodgers, the author of *Vegetarian Meals for People On-the-Go* (Hay House, 2002), if you simply can't avoid eating non-organic fruits and vegetables, wash them with Bragg's apple cider vinegar—it's a wonderful, and natural, pesticide remover.

- **Toxins in beverages.** The angels ask us to eliminate or significantly reduce alcohol, caffeine, and carbonation from our diet. Drink spring water, not "drinking water," as the angels urge us to drink water in as natural a form as possible. Drink fresh fruit juice, as the life force in fruits leaves 20 minutes after it's squeezed. Concentrated or refrigerated fruit juice has healthful vitamins, but it is not as life-giving as freshly squeezed juice.

- **Nitrates.** Avoid cured meats, such as lunch meats, sausage, and bacon. There are wonderful substitutes made of soy products that look, taste, and smell like the real thing. Many supermarkets carry these deli-substitute products, as do most health-food stores.

- **Toxins in toiletry items.** Avoid laurel sodium sulphate, a nitrate catalyst; and propylene glycol, an industrial antifreeze. Read the labels on your lotions, toothpastes, makeup, and shampoos. Weleda makes one of the only toothpastes that

doesn't have laurel sodium sulphate as an ingredient (their "Plant Gel" and "Calendula" toothpastes are wonderful and can be ordered at
800-241-1030), and Aubrey makes great additive-
free lotions (1-800-AUBREYH). Health-food
stores carry a wide variety of nontoxic products,
but be sure to read the ingredient labels, because
some so-called natural products contain laurel
sodium sulphate and other toxins.

- **Toxins in household products.** Avoid cocamide
  DEA, DEA, sodium laurel sulfate, sodium laureth
  sulfate, tallow, and synthetic fragrance. Health-
  food stores carry natural and effective cleaners
  and detergents. Avoid bleach and bleached paper
  products, such as napkins and paper towels.

- **Pollutants.** If you smoke, ask your angels to help
  release you from the cravings. Avoid fumes and
  secondhand smoke. Make sure to open the windows of your home and office daily to keep air
  circulating. When choosing where to live, work,
  shop, or play, pay attention to pollutant factors.
  For instance, when I was house-shopping once,
  the angels clearly told me to not choose a house
  because it was too close to Pacific Coast High-
  way. "It will poison you to be that close to ex-
  haust fumes," they clearly told me.

You can accelerate your detoxification process by
drinking plenty of fluids and by getting adequate sleep,

exercise, and fresh air. Drinking "wheat grass juice," which most juice bars and health-food stores offer, can also pull metals and pollutants out of your body rapidly.

At the risk of sounding extremely esoteric, the angels say that they're working with us to increase the "vibrational frequency" of our bodies. Like a violin string that vibrates at a higher rate according to the note that's played, we're beginning to move up the scale ourselves. We're doing so to keep pace with Earth's accelerated vibrational frequency.

This doesn't mean that we move faster during the day, or that we become busier or more rushed. Vibrational frequency means that we're less dense and more sensitive to the higher, finer frequencies of the angelic realm. It means that we're more intuitive, creative, and naturally energized.

If you feel compelled to eliminate certain foods or beverages from your diet, mentally ask your guardian angels to heal your cravings (and those of your Indigos) so that you won't miss the product. You'll be amazed at how easily you can give up toxic foods and drinks if you'll ask the angels to assist you. Every week, I meet people who tell me that the angels eliminated or significantly reduced their cravings for alcohol, sugar, white bread, chocolate, colas, nicotine, and other toxins. I had the same experience myself, where my cravings for junk food and coffee were completely removed.

Here's a wonderful prayer to say:

> *"Dear angels, please surround me with your healing energy, and help me to heal away my cravings for unhealthful foods and drinks. Please remove my desire for toxic substances, and help me have the motivation to live and eat healthfully. Please guide me while shopping, preparing, and eating food, and give me guidance*

about how to live without polluting myself or my world.
With great love and gratitude, I thank you."

Indigo Children and Animals

Due to their intuitive nature, Indigo Children usually develop close bonds with their pets. Unspoken, telepathic communication between children and animals is common. Giving your kids the opportunity to raise and care for a pet can help them grow in many ways.

For example, a woman named Jennifer, who has attended several of my workshops, told me how a pet rabbit affected her Indigo Child, Shelby. Jennifer told me:

> My six-year-old daughter, Shelby, is very sensitive. We lost a pet last year, a beloved domesticated rabbit named Belle. When Belle passed on, Shelby, her older sister, Missy, and I had a funeral for her. During the funeral, we discussed God, heaven, and whether we would ever see Belle the rabbit again.
>
> Shelby did her best to console Missy, who was very upset. Shelby showed no grief, not even a tear. This concerned me until she mentioned to Missy, "Belle doesn't want you to be sad; can't you see her? She's not sick anymore, and she sent you angels to make you feel better and not be sad."
>
> I was shocked, but pleased, upon hearing this information. Shelby truly believed the angels were there and described them in detail. All of this was comforting to Missy. Shelby still talks to Belle and the angels, and death has become a less frightening experience for all of us.

Pets definitely enhance our lives. However, parental supervision is often necessary to ensure that your children keep their commitment to walk and feed the dog, or change the cat's litter box daily. Sometimes, Indigo Children lose interest in their pets and pass the responsibility along to their parents. A wise parent firmly, but lovingly, discusses the commitment that the kids made to the pet. This teaches the Indigo Children about long-term commitments, which will be a useful mind-set to have when they approach marriage and parenthood.

Teaching your children to be kind to animals is an investment in their future. Studies show that violent criminals often have a childhood history of animal cruelty. When I walk on the beach, I sometimes see a child or teenager running after seagulls. From the expression on their face, I see that they're enjoying chasing the birds into flight. What the children don't realize, however, is that their actions are terrifying the birds.

I always make it a point to stop and talk to any kids who are chasing the seagulls. I explain that the birds are our friends and that we shouldn't frighten them. I can usually tell, from these conversations, that I'm probably the first adult who has ever discussed animal treatment with them. I wish that all parents would do this at home.

On a related note, if your children say that they want to become vegetarian due to their love for animals, don't worry about their protein or nutritional intake. Becky Prelitz, a registered dietitian and the co-author of our book *Eating in the Light* (Hay House, 2001) explains that vegetarians get adequate amounts of protein, vitamins, and minerals as long as they supplement with vitamins, minerals, and animal substitutes such as beans, nuts, soy milk, and tofu.

Indigo Children and Environmentalism

Indigo Children, like lightworkers, have a Life Purpose to help the world. You can help your Indigos heal any sense

of emptiness and to feel like they're making a positive difference by teaching them some simple methods.

For instance, when you and your children go for nature
walks, bring along a bag. Pick up litter (especially plastic and
metal, which take a long time to biodegrade) along the way.
Also, teach your kids to recycle household and kitchen items.
Ask your Indigos to rinse out salad-dressing bottles and other
recyclables that need cleaning prior to disposal into the re-
cycling bin. Be creative when thinking of even more ways
you and your kids can contribute to the healing of Mother
Earth.

❧❧❧ ❧❧❧

✺ Chapter Nine ✺

Food and the Indigo Child's Mood

If you're like most parents, you've noticed that your children's moods and energy levels are affected by the foods they eat and the beverages they drink. Foods with additives, such as preservatives and food coloring, have a measurable effect on ADHD symptoms, according to a double-blind study conducted by Dr. Marvin Boris, a pediatrician at a New York hospital. After the study, Boris concluded:

> Dietary factors may play a significant role in the etiology of the majority of children with ADHD. It makes a lot more sense to try modifying a children's diet before treating him or her with a stimulant drug. Health organizations and professionals should recognize that avoiding certain foods and additives can greatly benefit some troubled children.

In a London study of 78 children with ADHD symptoms, researchers disguised food containing sugar, additives, and dyes so that it looked "natural." By doing so, researchers could tell if the children's expectations about a food being processed triggered their hyperactive behavior. Yet, the children who ate processed food, whether it was disguised or not, all exhibited hyperactivity immediately afterward. The researchers concluded the study by urging doctors and clinicians to believe parents when they reported that food changed their children's behavior.

The Indigo Children Know

Indigo Children have a strong inner drive to feel happy, healthy, and peaceful. They don't *want* to be hyperactive or lethargic, but they also don't know what steps to take to feel better. So, they opt for short-term fixes that will temporarily soothe their minds and bodies.

Indigo Children who experiment with nutritious foods usually become self-motivated to keep eating healthfully. They just need us adults to teach them about, and give them access to, such foods. I'm deeply concerned that fast-food restaurants cater the lunches of most public schools. However, children who have learned that fast food leads to low energy and negative feelings will opt to bring a healthful lunch from home.

Indigo Child Alec recalls how his former bad diet negatively affected him: "I used to eat tons of candy, and I was depleted all the time; I had no energy and I was always tired. I was very moody, and the slightest thing would make me happy or sad. I felt like I didn't really have control over myself. I was depressed a lot, and I didn't realize why. Now that I eat more fruits and vegetables, my moods are better."

After experimenting with various eating styles, Alec decided that he felt best on a vegetarian diet. He says, "Meat makes me heavy and dull feeling. It makes me more aggressive. I've read that when the animal is killed, it gets an adrenaline rush. When you eat it, you get some of that."

Another Indigo Child, Christopher, reports that he had similar findings about how his meals have affected him:

> When I was younger, my parents fed me hamburgers and french fries from McDonald's and other fast-food restaurants. Eating fast food all the time as a child set me up to hurry and rush through life! Now I've learned that while pizza tastes good, I feel so bad afterwards. It makes my tummy hurt, and I get grumpy unless I go out dancing afterwards to discharge the negative energy. I really like smoothies and juice drinks. They make me feel good, and they give me lots of energy.

Christopher thinks that Ritalin would be unnecessary if children would change their diet. He says:

> I think that the kids who are taking Ritalin need to eat a more balanced diet of whole foods. I think that will help solve the problem. I think that ADD is caused by a poor, unbalanced diet. Too much sugar and caffeine.

Christopher has seen, firsthand, the negative effects that unhealthful eating has had on him and his friends at school. He goes on to say:

> I feel that there are better solutions, other than Ritalin. I think that a more balanced diet will help focus your attention, especially if you eliminate refined white sugar and flour.
>
> Yes, I think that ADD exists, but I think that it comes from a poor diet and having too much of a rush of energy rather than a slow, gradual release of energy. It makes it very difficult to concentrate if you have the high peaks of energy that you get from refined foods like white sugar. A more balanced diet will help to fix this problem. Ritalin is not necessary.
>
> When I'm eating fresh fruits and vegetables and as much *live* food as possible, I feel really good. I have a lot of

energy when I eat this way. Whenever I eat large amounts of cooked food, or if I drink large amounts of alcohol, I don't feel good.

Another Indigo Child named Ryan agrees. He says that he never noticed how much his diet affected his mood until he went to an acupuncturist:

> The acupuncturist put me on a diet without any false or bleached sugars. After I did it for a long time and then would go back to eating those things, I noticed that I wouldn't feel right. You're putting something unnatural in your body, and your body doesn't run right like that. After I started eating natural foods and healthy stuff, I noticed that processed foods and bleached and unnatural foods really affect how I feel.

Many children (and adults) stay away from health foods because they associate it with a flavorless and bland diet. Yet, this type of food has become absolutely delicious and flavorful in the last decade, especially with the rich new influx of organic foods and meat substitutes that are now available.

We're fortunate to live in a time when there are both large and small health-food stores are in most metropolitan and suburban areas. Many of these stores have delis and restaurants so that you can eat healthfully without having to be a gourmet chef. My book *Eating in the Light* offers tips on how to introduce vegetarian and healthful foods into your family's daily meals.

The Spiritual Energy of Food

Your Indigo Children are exquisitely sensitive to flavor, smell, and texture, so they're bound to be picky eaters. Fortunately, they can turn this sensitivity into an asset by tuning in to their body's mood and energy fluctuations. If, like Alec, Christopher, and Ryan, they can notice the link between how they feel and how they eat, then they'll become internally motivated to eat better.

Your Indigo Children's spiritual nature creates an internal push, which urges them to live at a high spiritual "frequency." The higher someone's frequency, the more accomplished they are with respect to their psychic and spiritual healing abilities. You can support their Life Purpose by helping them elevate their spiritual frequency. A major contribution to this endeavor is through teaching your Indigos about the spiritual energy of food.

Everything has a "life force," which could be thought of as the way in which atoms move around. Food is no exception. Some food has more life force than other foods. When a vegetable or fruit is still on the tree or vine and reaches its ripeness, its life force is at its highest. If you eat this freshly picked, vine-ripened fruit or vegetable, you're consuming a large dose of life force. As a result, you'll notice that your energy and mood will be positively boosted right after you eat it. The more high life-force foods that your Indigo Children eat, the higher their spiritual frequency will be.

The factors that reduce life force in foods include:

- **Cooking, freezing, canning, freeze-drying, microwaving, and steaming.** Anything that would kill the life force in a human also kills the life force in fruits, grains, and vegetables. If in doubt, ask yourself, "Could I survive the process that I'm putting this food through?" If your answer is no, then know that the food's life force is being disrupted, too.

- **Blending and juicing.** The life force only stays in fruits and vegetables for 20 minutes after they're juiced. That's why fresh fruit juice is infinitely better for your Indigo Children than canned or bottled.

- **Additives.** Sugar, white flour, food dyes, and preservatives have all been correlated with ADHD behaviors. These additives also have no life force, and they rob healthful foods of their life force as well.

- **Pesticides.** Pesticide means "kill," and this aggressive energy is found in fruit, vegetables, grains, and oils unless we take steps to remove the residue. Meat purchased at a supermarket is filled with these pesticides. It's much better to only buy organic foods and cooking supplies, or free-range meat, in the first place. Even though they cost more, your other expenses will be reduced (such as medication, health-care treatments, psychological care, compulsive-spending costs, junk food purchases, and weight-loss treatments). Plus, organic food tastes so much better than ordinary produce that your children will be motivated to eat the food that would normally spoil from non-usage.

Take your children with you to a meeting of a local vegetarian or environmental society (see Resources section for information on how to contact the groups nearest you). Often, our Indigo Children respond better to listening to food facts from an outside authority than a parent. Yet, our children ultimately learn about eating habits by watching us adults.

And remember, if *you* are a lightworker, you too will benefit from eating a diet of high life-force food.

Hypoglycemic or ADHD?

"Low blood sugar, or hypoglycemia, is the most significant underlying problem I find in children who exhibit behavioral problems," says Mary Ann Block, D.O., P.A., the author of *No More Ritalin*. She lists the behavioral symptoms of hypoglycemia as "the child who is agitated or irritable when he or she wakes up in the morning, or before meals, and then is better after eating; and the child with the Jekyll and Hyde behavior, who is sweet and fine one minute, and then for no apparent reason, is agitated, angry, and irritable the next."

Dr. Block says, "The treatment for hypoglycemia is simple: Change the child's diet. Make sure that the child never gets hungry, and eliminate refined carbohydrates, such as candy, cakes, pies, and soft drinks from [their] diet."

My Indigo son Chuck experiences hypoglycemia when he goes too long without eating. On his own, Chuck has discovered how to keep his blood sugar high by eating frequent, small, and healthful snacks. He avoids caffeine, chocolate, and sugar. When his blood sugar drops, Chuck becomes tired and irritable. But he recognizes that his low mood and energy is temporary and food related, so he doesn't buy into it. He simply takes it as a signal to eat. Once he does so, his energy level and mood return to their normal state very quickly.

I agree with Dr. Block's advice about making sure that your hypoglycemic-prone children don't become hungry, even if it seems inconvenient. She writes:

It is best that the child with the symptoms of hypo-glycemia go no longer than two hours without eating. If your child has this problem and tells you she is hungry, but dinner will be ready in thirty minutes, it is tempting to have her wait for dinner. I strongly suggest that you find some-thing for your child to eat right then. Don't make her wait for dinner. When children with hypoglycemia get hungry, they need to eat now!

Dr. Block suggests giving children a small snack of trail mix, nuts, or a peanut butter sandwich, which will quickly stabilize their blood sugar without ruining their appetite for dinner.

What's for Breakfast?

It's a cliché that breakfast is the most important meal of the day. Yet, for children with ADHD symptoms, it's a tru-ism with major effects. Studies consistently show that chil-dren who eat breakfast have better test scores, school attendance, and attention spans; as well as less depression and hyperactivity. So, if your Indigo Children eat breakfast—especially a healthful one—you'll probably see significant improvements in their moods, energy levels, and ability to concentrate.

A recent survey showed that 79 percent of eight- and nine-year-old children eat breakfast daily. That's not too bad, although I wish it was closer to 100 percent. Yet, when chil-dren get older, they may be more apt to skip breakfast. The same survey found that only 58 percent of 12- and 13-year-olds ate breakfast regularly.

You can help your Indigo Children start the day off right by stocking the pantry and refrigerator with a healthful selec-tion of breakfast foods. If your children want to eat leftovers from dinner for breakfast, it's better than if they skip breakfast. And leftover pizza is an infinitely better breakfast than a bowl of sugar-and-food-dye-filled commercial breakfast cereal!

Catherine, my Indigo stepdaughter, doesn't like to eat breakfast, yet when she skips this meal, she's irritable and cranky. She also knows that she needs to take a vitamin-and-mineral supplement daily (which is a good idea for every Indigo Child). However, Catherine has difficulty swallowing large vitamin pills.

We've solved the problem by keeping the ingredients for smoothies in our home. That way, she can make a quick and healthful breakfast. We buy protein powder at the health-food store, making sure that it's supplemented with vitamins and minerals. We also make sure that it's fruit-sweetened and doesn't contain sugar, food dye, or preservatives.

Catherine puts cold vanilla soy milk, a banana, and a scoop of protein powder into the blender. In less than five minutes, she's got a breakfast drink to take with her to school.

Other ideas for quick and healthy breakfast foods include the following:

- Tofu scrambles (take soft tofu and scramble it like eggs, mixing it with your favorite omelet ingredients)
- Whole-grain toast or a bagel with peanut butter and sugar-free fruit spread
- Soy bacon or sausage (it tastes remarkably similar to meat)
- Whole grain, fruit-sweetened cereal, topped with fresh fruit
- Yogurt with fresh fruit and chopped nuts

- Frozen whole-grain waffles (just pop them in the toaster)
- Fruit salad
- A breakfast burrito

Breakfast ingredients to avoid include anything with refined sugar, food dye, preservatives, caffeine, and artificial sweeteners. You can teach your children to read the ingredient labels of food and beverages so that they'll become informed consumers.

When my son Grant was younger, I taught him to read labels and to specifically avoid "phosphoric acid." This common ingredient in colas and food leaches magnesium from our body whenever we eat or drink it. Scientist Kenneth Weaver, M.D., of East Tennessee State University, found that each 12-ounce can of cola contains 36 milligrams of phosphoric acid, and the result is that 36 milligrams of magnesium are removed from the body. As you'll soon read, most Indigo Children have magnesium deficiencies.

Wanting to prevent Grant from having a magnesium deficiency, I gave him one dollar a day for every day that he avoided eating or drinking products containing phosphoric acid. The result was amazing and definitely well worth my seven dollars a week!

I'd watch him spontaneously read labels of food and drinks as we'd go grocery shopping together. He began drinking fruit-flavored water instead of soda, and he'd avoid preservatives altogether, instead of just phosphoric acid. Today, even though he's an adult and is no longer receiving money as an incentive, Grant still reads food and beverage labels to avoid ingesting phosphoric acid.

Supplements and ADHD Behavior

Researcher Stephen Schoenthaler, who has studied inmate, juvenile delinquent, and school populations extensively, found that children's IQ's rise, and their delinquent behavior significantly drops, after they take vitamin and mineral supplements. Another researcher, Dr. Richard Carlton, found that vitamin and mineral supplements lead to significant improvements in academics and behavior.

Carlton reported, "Some children gained three to five years in reading comprehension within the first year of treatment, and all children in special education classes became mainstreamed, and their grades rose significantly." When some of the students whom Carlton was studying stopped taking vitamins and minerals, there was an immediate decline in their grades. Carlton also noted that the students taking vitamins and mineral supplements became more sociable and exhibited better moods.

The supplement ingredients that helped students the most were magnesium, vitamin B-6, vitamin C, thiamine, folic acid, and zinc. It was found that *manganese* (not to be confused with *magnesium*) caused irritability and difficulty concentrating in some students, so the researchers removed it from the study.

Children who are hyperactive have lower serotonin levels than children who aren't hyperactive, according to a study published in the *Pediatrics Journal*. Low serotonin can result in lethargy, depression, and food cravings. When the researchers gave hyperactive children some vitamin B-6, their serotonin levels significantly increased. Another study compared the serotonin levels for children who received vitamin B-6 with another group of children who received

Ritalin. Only the B-6 group showed elevated serotonin levels, and these positive results lasted long after the group stopped receiving B-6.

Children who received magnesium supplements showed a significant decrease in hyperactivity, compared to control groups who received placebos in a study of children ages 7 through 12. Since colas and many processed foods contain phosphoric acid, which leaches magnesium from the body, it's essential that you read food labels and steer clear of phosphoric acid.

One study found that 95 percent of ADHD children were deficient in magnesium. Another found that not only did ADHD children lack sufficient magnesium levels, but they were also deficient in iron, copper, and calcium. The researchers concluded, "It is necessary to supplement trace elements in children with hyperactivity." In other words, we must make sure that children who are hyperactive get daily vitamin and mineral supplements that contain magnesium, iron, copper, and calcium.

Fatty Acids and Behavior

Many new studies show that children labeled ADHD also have essential fatty acid deficiencies. You've probably seen bottles of "flaxseed oil" in the refrigerators at health-food stores, and may have wondered what they were for. Well, many people are supplementing their diets with one capful of flaxseed oil daily. This is an easy way to ensure that you have a sufficient amount of essential fatty acids.

Symptoms of essential fatty-acid deficiencies include excessive thirst, frequent urination, dry patches of skin, and miniature whiteheads on the backs of the arms. One study found that 40 percent of boys with ADHD symptoms also had these symptoms. Some experts believe that ADHD behavior is a symptom of essential fatty-acid deficiency.

It's so easy to correct this deficiency! Simply purchase flaxseed oil, hempseed oil, or soy oil. Pour one teaspoon daily in your children's salad, smoothie, or other foods. And while you're at it, make sure that you put a teaspoon in your own meals. Your hair and skin will shine with new luster, making it definitely worth the extra calories and fat grams!

Food Dye, Sugar, Preservatives, and Additives

Food dye, sugar, and preservatives have been scientifically linked to ADHD and ADD behaviors. At least 17 double-blind studies have linked food dye with hyperactivity and insomnia, especially in young children. In one study, 150 of 200 children (75 percent) slept better and were less irritable and restless after synthetic food coloring was removed from their diet. Another study showed that children had improved behavior after changing to a food-dye free diet, and that the improvement was long-lasting.

Sugar has been a controversial factor in the ADHD equation. Some studies showed no link between sugar and hyperactive behavior, and those studies received a lot of media fanfare. Yet, when you look at the methodology of studies that refute sugar's role in creating hyperactivity, you see confounding variables. However, the studies that are tightly controlled for these factors consistently reveal a strong correlation between sugar consumption and hyperactivity. And most parents will tell you that they see definite changes in their children's behavior after they eat dessert.

For example, Yale University researchers gave refined

white sugar to children and compared their blood adrenaline levels before and after sugar consumption. They discovered that the amount of adrenaline soared ten times higher following consumption of the sugar! Adrenaline, as you know, is the heart-pumping chemical that prepares you for combat or dangerous situations. So, no wonder our children run around screaming their heads off after they eat a candy bar! If that wasn't bad enough, the Yale scientists also found that the children were irritable, anxious, and had difficulty concentrating, after sugar consumption.

Other university studies found a link between aggressiveness, antisocial behavior in children, and sugar consumption. When schools in New York banned food dyes and additives from school lunches, they experienced the most dramatic rise in academic performance for any school district ever recorded.

Two studies of imprisoned violent and aggressive young people showed a dramatic (47 to 77 percent) drop in the number of aggressive and criminal acts, as well as suicide attempts, when sugar and food additives were removed from the inmates' meals.

It's not okay to rationalize, "Well, a little bit of food dye won't hurt my children." One study examined the hyperactivity of children after they ate just one cookie containing food dye. Within one hour of eating the one cookie, the children showed increased hyperactivity. Another study found decreased performance in hyperactive students within hours of ingesting food dye.

When I related the results of these studies to a woman named Tammy whose two sons were ADHD, she said, "Wow, I'll bet all the fast food that we eat really is contributing to their problems!" I was glad that Tammy saw the connection, so I was saddened and surprised by what she said next.

"But what else can I do?" Tammy shrugged her shoulders. "I'm so busy with the kids that when dinner time rolls around, all I have the time and energy for is fast food."

I listened to Tammy compassionately, remembering how I felt when my two sons were young. Then, I gently asked, "If your children were calmer and less active, would you feel less drained of energy and time?"

"Of course," she nodded.

"Well, let me suggest an experiment," I said. "You live only a couple miles from a major health-food store that has a really nice delicatessen. They have wonderful, delicious cooked dinner foods in their deli. So, you can buy healthful fast food that you, your husband, and children will truly enjoy. Try eating that way for a week, and let me know what happens, okay?"

"But isn't health food a lot more expensive? We're on a really tight budget, you know." Tammy countered.

"In some ways, it might be more expensive to buy organic and healthful food. But let me ask you: Do you think that your children's hyperactivity is costing you money in other ways? Like medication, or buying things to 'make them happy'? And what about the cost of peacefulness in the household, and the effect on your marriage?"

Tammy told me that she'd give it a try. When I next saw her, she gave me a big hug. "I can't believe the difference this has made!" she said. "The kids are much happier and calmer, which has definitely helped the relationship between my husband and me. Finally, I can get them to go to bed on time, and they now sleep through the night! I never knew how much our eating habits were affecting everything. I wish I'd tried this years ago!" Tammy patted her belly, which carried her soon-to-be-born baby. "This one will be raised on healthy food from day one! " she said.

I told Tammy that I'd seen similar positive effects when I began preparing organic meals for my sons. Since my oldest son and husband still ate meat, I switched from buying the supermarket variety to purchasing only free-range meat at health-food stores.

"Meat from the supermarket is loaded with hormones and pesticides that affect your family's health and behavior," I explained to Tammy. "Those animals are mistreated throughout their lives. They're raised in tiny little pens where they can't even lie down or turn around. Then, their slaughter is something straight out of a horror movie. All of their pain and misery creates an energy that's part of their flesh. When we eat meat from supermarkets, we're literally eating the energy of pain. It lowers our energy frequency.

"Commercial farmers give their livestock growth hormones to increase the animals' size. But studies show that these hormones stay in the meat, and when we eat the meat, we're eating hormones that could produce aggressiveness in us. The animals eat grain that's loaded with pesticides, and these pesticides are transferred into the animals' flesh and dairy products.

"Then, there are the environmental issues! We're on the verge of having water shortages. And the largest consumption of water comes from raising cows for meat, dairy, and leather products. It takes 2,500 gallons of water to produce just one pound of beef. Since there are so many alternatives to beef, milk, and leather, we feel like we're contributing to Mother Earth by avoiding products made from cows.

"My sons became gentler and less aggressive when I began feeding them organic produce and free-range meat and dairy products. They seemed more accessible, and I noticed that we began to connect emotionally on a deeper level. I feel that they became more compassionate just through that one change in our diet."

Ayurveda and Indigo Children's Eating Patterns

Alec Bridges, a student and teacher of Ayurveda, is also an Indigo Child. I thought he would be particularly qualified to discuss how you can better understand your Indigo Children by getting to know their constitution, as defined by Ayurveda. Here is what he shares with us:

> Ayurveda is the medical system that evolved out of the meditative states of the minds of the ancient seers of truth, or *rishis*, of India about 5,000 years ago. There is an infinite amount of wisdom within Ayurveda (the literal translation is "science of life"), but I'll just talk about what is relevant here.
>
> According to Ayurveda, there are three basic constitutions, or *doshas*. They are based on the five elements: ether (space), air, fire, water, and earth. The three doshas are: vata, pitta, and kapha. Everybody has a certain degree of all three of the doshas within them, but usually one or two of them are dominant. Each person is born with their own unique mixture of vata, pitta, and kapha. This configuration is called Prakruti. The literal translation of Prakruti is "nature." To get the most out of your life, it is best to stay in balance with your Prakruti.

Vata. The vata dosha is made up of the ether and air elements. People of a vata constitution will usually have a very quick and creative mind. They learn new things very fast, but they also forget things as quickly as they learn them. Vata is the principle of motion and is essential for all bodily and mental functions to take place, but when out of balance, this aspect of vata leans toward ungroundedness. The attributes of vata are: dry, light (light as in lightweight), cold, rough, subtle, mobile, clear, and dispersing. The time of year that vata is at its highest is fall. Whenever there is a lot of dryness in the air, or it is very windy or cold, a vata person has to be especially careful.

When in balance, a vata person is very clear-minded, creative, inspired, and flexible. When out of balance, a vata person will tend to get nervous, will suffer from anxiety and fear, will worry, will be forgetful, and will have a very scattered mind (this is important in relation to ADHD). If you have excessive gas, this is a good indication that vata is out of balance. The main site for vata in the body is the abdomen, most specifically the large intestine; this is where the gas will come from.

Another area of vata is the low back, so vatas have to be careful of this area. Another important vata area is any joint in the body. Joints are where movement occurs, so vata—being the principle of movement—is high in joints. Most types of arthritis are from high vata in the joints. It is important to do simple, repetitive movements in every joint in your body every day to avoid arthritis. Also, flaxseed oil is particularly good for keeping joints well lubricated and healthy, and it is good for vatas in general.

Enough about imbalance. Let's talk about how to get vata back into balance. Basically you apply the opposite of whatever vata attribute is out of balance. For example, if you are feeling very dry, then drink water. If you are cold, then eat something spicy or put on a jacket.

Here are some things you can do to keep vata in balance:

- Keep warm. Eat foods that are warming. (*The Ayurvedic Cookbook* by Amandea Morningstar and Urmila Desai has tons of great recipes for balancing all of the doshas.)
- Go easy on raw food and beans.
- Warm, moist, and oily food is very good for vatas, as is sesame oil and ghee (clarified butter).
- Foods with sweet, sour, and salty flavors are the best for vatas, as long as the sweets come from natural fruit-sweetened sources and are not from refined white sugar.
- Live in a warm, humid climate, such as the tropics.
- Be moderate with your sexual energy—this is mainly for males. Depleted sexual energy leads to very low vitality and an extremely dull and tired mind. Vatas usually will have the least amount of sexual energy of the three doshas, and they lose it the easiest.
- Last but definitely not least, *keep a regular schedule and routine*. Vatas tend to go whichever way the wind blows and this, in excess, will throw them out of balance like nothing else.

Vatas are usually very slight and slender. They often have darker features than the other doshas. They usually have the least powerful digestive fire, so eating foods that are easy to digest is very helpful in keeping them balanced. Vatas also tire much sooner than the other doshas, but ironically are the first ones to jump up and start whatever it is that is going on. This is another thing to be aware of: Know when enough is enough. Vatas will always want to do something. They tend to be very restless, but sometimes, if they just stay home and rest, they will find that they will start having more energy. Vata is always the first thing to go out of balance in the body, so people with a lot of vata have to be extra careful.

Pitta. The pitta dosha is made up of the elements of fire and water. Pitta attributes are hot, oily, sharp, and penetrating, light (as in bright light), mobile, liquid, and sour-smelling.

Usually, the most obvious thing about pittas is their hot and fiery quality. When out of balance, they tend toward anger, jealousy, fierce competitiveness, and basically Type A behavior. When in balance, they are great leaders, they love to take charge of themselves and sometimes others, they are very organized, they are very determined, and they have great willpower.

The time of year that pitta is at its highest is late spring and summer. Pitta thrives in cool, dry climates.

Pitta is the principle of digestion and absorption. The main pitta place in the body is the stomach and small intestines. When in balance, this serves for very good digestion and absorption, but when out of balance, it can be felt as an acidic stomachache and can lead to ulcers.

Here are some things you can do to balance pitta:

- Keep cool.
- Live in a cool, dry climate.
- Avoid excess oils, fried foods, caffeine, salt, alcohol, red meat, and hot spices.
- Eat lots of fresh fruits and vegetables.
- Avoid foods with a sour, salty, and/or pungent flavor.
- Eat foods with the sweet, bitter, and astringent flavors.
- Learn to express your feelings in a positive and constructive way.

A pitta person usually has a medium body frame and a very athletic body. Their features are light, they have blond or red hair, fair skin, blue or green eyes, and freckles. They have a good amount of stamina and vitality, and they need it since they are so driven.

Watch out when a pitta has not eaten for a while; their strong digestive fire can turn into irritability or anger really quickly if there is no food to soak it up.

The most relevant thing with pitta and ADHD is their expression of emotions. This is very important for pitta. If their creative expression is suppressed, the unexpressed emotion can turn into an ulcer or a boiling cauldron of rage. Let your children express themselves. It's important that the expression is constructive and positive. Imbalanced pitta is prone to anger, so this is something to watch out for. Anger, at the level of vocal or physical expression, rarely does the world any good. Get your pitta under control and express positively. Pittas are just as capable of love and intense inspiration as they are of anger and jealousy.

Kapha. Kapha is made up of the elements of earth and water. Their main attributes are: heavy, slow, cold, oily, slimy, dense, soft, and static. People with kapha constitutions have a larger body frame. There is a strong tendency for kaphas to carry excess weight. They have a fair and bright complexion, with soft and oily skin. They usually have thick, dark, oily, and wavy hair; and their eyes are large, dark, and beautiful.

Kapha people, when in balance, are very grounded. When out of balance, they are too grounded. They can suffer from inertia, depression, overall lack of motivation, and they will sleep too much. Of all the doshas, kapha needs the least amount of sleep, but they are the ones who like to sleep the most.

They are blessed with strength, tons of stamina, and overall high vitality when they are balanced. They are generally slow learners, but once they do learn something, they rarely forget it. They are good at earning, and holding on to, money. They tend toward greed and attachment. This is because of the energy that they have. It's hard for them to lose weight and difficult for them to let go of things in general. They can be very stubborn and set in their ways. When in balance, kapha people are very reliable, loving, full of compassion, strong, grounded, disciplined, and enduring.

Here are some things to do to keep kapha in balance:

- Get plenty of physical activity every day. Kaphas are the most capable of strenuous exercise.
- Go easy on foods that are high in fat, and avoid fried foods.
- Eat foods that are warm, light, and dry.
- Avoid foods with the sweet, salty, and sour flavors.
- Eat foods with a pungent, bitter, and/or astringent taste. Raw salads are great for kaphas.
- Don't be afraid of change and excitement.

The time of year when kapha is at its highest is the winter and early spring. This is the most important time of year for kaphas to watch their diet. Kaphas will feel most balanced if they live in a dry, hot climate such as the desert.

I think the most relevant thing for kaphas and ADHD is their lack of motivation and inertia. The best thing for this is to get plenty of exercise every day. Yoga is great for kaphas, but not gentle yoga. Something like Ashtanga or Bikram's yoga is perfect once you get used to doing yoga. Kaphas have the most strength and stamina, so they can do vigorous exercise much easier than vatas or pittas.

Another good thing for kaphas is waking up early and going to bed early. Too much sleep will make them feel just as tired, if not more tired, than not enough sleep. Staying up late, though, is not the answer.

Handling and Healing Food Cravings

One of the reasons why people may avoid health food is their belief that healthful food is tasteless, bland, or boring. Many well-intentioned people give in to their cravings for sweets and junk food, not realizing that there are delicious and healthful alternatives.

I spent my first decade as a psychotherapist treating people with eating disorders. I directed outpatient and inpatient eating-disorder clinics and wrote several books on the subject. My doctoral dissertation was on the link between child abuse and the development of eating disorders, work that became the basis for my book *Losing Your Pounds of Pain* (Hay House, 1994).

My book *Constant Craving* (Hay House, 1995) delves into all of the scientific and empirical research on food cravings. It explains the physical, emotional, and spiritual reasons why we crave certain foods.

Here's what I wrote about sugar cravings:

> Several researchers have studied the innate desire for sweets in human infants. Newborn infants were presented with a choice of sweetened fluid and plain water. Which liquid do you suppose the babies preferred? Even one-day-old infants drank more when given sweet fluids. Not only that, but the sweeter the concentration of fluids, the more liquid the babies consumed. Many researchers conclude, from studies such as this, that we have an innate preference for sweets.
>
> Our human appetite for sweets may have arisen in our ancient primate ancestors. Monkeys and other primates show a preference for sweet fruits over any other type of food. Some researchers speculate that fruits were a sure source of calories and energy for our cave-dwelling ancestors, and we developed a natural affinity for sweet stuff as a result of survival instincts. Along the same lines, we "knew" that sweetness equated ripeness when we were foraging for food in the wild. All animals, in fact, prefer sweets over other types of foods. Studies with horses, bears, and ants show a universal love for sugary-sweet foods.
>
> Our instincts to seek out sweet-tasting fruit have been bastardized today, twisted in an appetite for candies. One reason for our "modern" cravings is the lack of truly sweet fruit at most grocery stores. We have a vast array of produce available

to us, but most of the selection is artificially ripened, tasteless, and not sufficiently sweet to satisfy us.

It's one more reason to shop at health-food stores, where fruit is tree-ripened and sweet. Organic produce always has more flavor, vitamins, and minerals than conventionally grown produce. Yes, it costs a little more, but how often has your conventional produce rotted in the refrigerator crisper because no one ate it? They didn't eat it because it was tasteless and unappetizing. But if you keep a bowl of organic berries, grapes, or carrots at eye level on your refrigerator shelf, your kids will be motivated to try it. Once they discover its taste, they'll keep eating it.

You'll also appreciate a big difference in how your children react when you take them with you to a health-food store. You won't have to deal with them screaming for the candy sold at most supermarket checkout stands because health-food stores have nutritious snacks for sale in that area. You also won't engage in power struggles with your children in the cereal aisle, as they beg for a cereal loaded with food dye and sugar.

Emotions, Cravings, and Angel Therapy

Eating can make us feel better, and many of our cravings represent an unconscious desire to self-medicate. Each food that we crave contains mood- and energy-altering properties that affect our brain's neurochemistry and our blood pressure and heart rate. When we crave a food or beverage, it's often because our body senses that we're imbalanced (because of an upsetting life situation, for instance). Our body craves a food that will create homeostasis, or balance.

When people tell me what food they crave, I know a lot about what's going on in their lives. There are predictable patterns linking certain food cravings to certain life issues. We can heal the food cravings by taking care of the life issue head-on. But if we ignore the life issue, our food cravings continue to haunt us.

Here are some common food cravings that Indigo Children have, along with the corresponding life issue. (A complete list of hundreds of food cravings and their meanings can be found in my book *Constant Craving*):

Food Craved	Meaning of Craving
Beer	Desire to shut out anxiety. Wanting more love, fun, and appreciation.
Cereal and Other Breakfast Foods	Procrastination, trying to avoid getting started with day's duties.
Cheeseburger	Frightened by a sense of inner emptiness or inadequacy, and feeling depression. Fear of failure.
Cheese (sharp)	Feeling exhausted and drained. A desire for comfort and renewal. Weariness.
Chips	You feel stressed or anxious, and you want to ease your worry. Also, a desire for validation.
Chocolate	Desire for romance and love.
Coffee	Energy drain from engaging in activities that are meaningless or intimidating to you. Burnout, resentment, or disappointment with your job.

Cola (diet)	A desire to feel full and energized. Also, a wish for exciting romantic feelings.
Cola (regular)	You're trying to stay motivated and energized, and you're combating internal stress.
Ice Cream	Trying to soothe and renew oneself due to depression.
French Fries	Feeling insecure or empty.
Nuts	Too much stress and not enough fun. Desiring playfulness.

Angel Therapy for Food Cravings

I was a chocolate addict for many years, and I ate it daily. I especially craved chocolate right before my menstrual cycle. When the angels told me that I needed to let go of chocolate so that I could elevate my spiritual frequency, I was sad and worried. They explained that the sugar and the stimulant phenylethylamine (P.E.A.) were blocking me from receiving high-level spiritual information. They said that chocolate was actually "pseudo-Divine love," and that I craved it because I was really craving God's love. That made sense to me, but I wondered how I could stop eating something when I craved it every day.

I told the angels, "I'd be happy to let go of chocolate if I didn't crave it so much." And they replied, "Are you asking us to help you heal your cravings?" I realized that the angels needed my permission before they could help me due to God's law of free will that states that not even the Creator can intervene unless we ask for help.

So I said to the angels, "Yes, please help and heal me. Please free me from chocolate cravings." The next day, I didn't want chocolate. I haven't wanted it at all since that day in 1996. Even when I went to see the movie *Chocolat*, I had zero desire for chocolate during or after the movie.

I've since taught this method to my students and audience members. Many people have told me that the angels healed their cravings for chocolate, alcohol, cigarettes, and other substances and behaviors that were interfering with their health or happiness.

You can send angels to your Indigo Children and request that these heavenly beings help heal your kids' cravings. The angels are "allowed" to intervene with other people to the degree that the situation involves you. Here's an example of a prayer:

> *"God and the healing angels, especially Archangel Raphael, I ask that you go to my children and release them from cravings for foods or substances that are interfering with their health, happiness, or Life Purpose. I ask for your intervention in this matter, to the degree that it affects me. I now surrender the entire situation to you, and know that it is already healed. Thank you."*

ネムネムネム ネネネ

⚜ *Chapter Ten* ⚜

Creative Outlets

Indigo Children, gifted children, children who are labeled ADD or ADHD, and adult lightworkers are almost always right-brain dominant. Scientific studies on the blood flow and activity of ADHD children's brains find that they use their visual center of the brain more than their logic-center lobe.

This means that they interact with the world primarily with the right hemisphere of their brain, which focuses upon visions and feelings and relates to nonverbal studies such as art, music, math, philosophy, psychology, and psychic arts. Right brain-dominant people can make excellent writers and speakers, provided they learn how to translate their mental pictures and strong internal feelings into words.

The left hemisphere, in contrast, is more concerned with words, and the left-brained person will be naturally proficient with grammar and vocabulary. The left-brained person is usually orderly and follows authority without question (and even welcomes it!).

The right-brained person is intuitive, only following "benevolent authority"—and then, only when they understand and trust the authority figure's motivation and goals. They learn by seeing, and do better with charts, graphs, slides, and demonstrations than by reading or listening to a lecture.

Because right-brained people have such acute senses, they're easily distracted. They can hear every little click of the school clock's hand, and the high-pitch sound of the fluorescent lighting. Jeffrey Freed, M.A.T., author of *Right-Brained Children in a Left-Brained World*, wrote about a boy named Herb who heard incredibly acutely. Like a person with a hearing aid turned up high, sounds were exaggerated to this boy. When a person talked in a normal conversational tone, Herb assumed that the person was yelling at him. This may explain why your Indigo Children become defensive when you talk with them.

Indigo Children and adult lightworkers usually hear a high-pitched ringing sound in one ear. This is a frequency sent by their guides and angels to help them. It helps to elevate their emotions and thoughts above the race-mind consciousness of problems. The sound also contains encoded information that is downloaded to them nonverbally. (By the way, if you find that you hear this sound and it bothers you, you can mentally ask your angels to turn down the volume, and they'll be happy to do so.)

Those who are hard of hearing often complain that their hearing aids are more of a curse than a boon. These devices cause them to hear everything simultaneously instead of just hearing the intended target. As a result, many people don't use their hearing aids. They choose to shut them off rather than being overwhelmed with noise. So, at a family gathering, these individuals may appear to be listless or unsociable. But what they really are is hard-of-hearing.

The same process is true with Indigo Children, who become overwhelmed with sights, sounds, and feelings. They shut down by withdrawing into introversion, or by acting-out aggressively.

Visual teaching aids work great with Indigo Children. Budget cuts have curtailed the arts programs at many schools, but many angelic teachers are diving into their own (often limited) pockets and paying for art supplies. Yet sometimes teachers are left-brained. That's how they excelled in school. These left-brained individuals are extremely organized, follow rules, and are focused listeners. They often assume that others learn in the same manner and that everyone would be happy if only they'd live an organized life. They don't realize that their methods are ineffective for people who process information visually.

Hungry for Creativity

Indigo Children need outlets to express their powerful energy. Exercise is one way to let the steam out so they don't explode like a pressure cooker. And creativity is another important means. In many of my sessions, the angels come through and suggest that Indigo Children get involved in some sort of creative venture. Any form will do: making beaded jewelry, decorating a bedroom, photography, dance, music, building sandcastles, doodling, or creative cooking.

Gabrielle Zale is an art and music therapist who has worked with children for 11 years. In 1995, Gabrielle opened an arts therapy unit at an adolescent residential treatment program, and she recalls how positively the arts affected the troubled teens at the facility:

> The children with whom I worked at the Residential Treatment Program, by every definition known today, were and are the Indigo Children. By helping them to express themselves creatively, I saw daily miracles happen with these children who were so abused and disturbed that they were normally unable to focus for just a few minutes.
>
> I found that the one aspect that the children wanted above anything else was peace. I found, also, that they needed more than anything to find the treasures buried deep within and express them through creativity and imagination . . . song, dance, painting, and acting. This alone began turning their behavior around.
>
> They created and painted all of their own props for a play I wrote for them about many of the great Native American chiefs. They sang beautiful folk and spiritual songs of peace and love. I had not expected them to embrace this type of music considering the heavy metal, hard-rock songs they were accustomed to, but I saw each one of them sing and dance from the heart.
>
> I also started seeing them become responsible and trustworthy as I entrusted to them the care of expensive equipment and props. These children took on the responsibility with joy and enthusiasm because I had placed my trust in them.
>
> The residential director asked me if I was becoming a "Pollyanna" because I never talked about negative points in the children. I told him that I hoped I was a Pollyanna because as I had heard Marianne Williamson once say, "Pollyanna was a miracle worker." She saw the best in others and that is what she got back from them.
>
> I find that Indigo Children respond to truth and detest the lies in our system. I have very firm boundaries with them, but I always also show empathy and compassion. I find that these children respect and respond to this type of correction and control.

If the Indigo Children's energy isn't focused in positive directions, it can be used in very negative, destructive ways, and that is what is happening in our schools today.

I have seen complete turnarounds in all of these Indigo Children when they are applying their creativity and imagination. They become absorbed and free-flowing. They lose almost all, if not all, of their moodiness and flow from the heart. They become compassionate and have an innate sense of working together as a whole. That is what I have observed in all these different projects that I have directed.

An Indigo Child named Dawn says that any type of creative expression, especially painting or listening to music, puts her in a good mood. She says that when she's being creative, her energy flows in a way that feels good to her.

As I mentioned earlier, Indigo Children seem to need a higher degree of stimulation than other kids do. Perhaps it's because the Indigos are wired for a tough mission. Regardless of why, though, the Indigo Children need healthy sources of stimulation such as music, gardening, yoga, singing, dancing, and so on. If Indigo Children don't have access to creative outlets and other healthy stimulation, they usually create their own form of stimulation. So, they may act-out to get attention, or create a high-drama crisis that makes them feel special.

The Indigo Children's Learning Style

Right-brain dominant people, such as Indigo Children and adult lightworkers, learn more by what they see than what they hear. Marianne told me that her Indigo son, Brad, wasn't doing well in school until she finally understood his visual learning style. She recalls:

He would try to learn his spelling list phonetically, and by saying or writing the words repeatedly. But no matter how much he tried, Brad couldn't get better than a C grade on his spelling tests.

Then I started talking to Brad about the way he processed information. Almost accidentally, I discovered that when Brad wants to remember something, he "sees" the memory in his mind's eye. This gave me an idea. Instead of helping Brad with rote memory, I began coaching him to memorize how his spelling words looked. The results were amazing!

On Brad's very next spelling test, he got 100 percent. I could tell that it really boosted his confidence, too. Now, he uses the same visual memorization method with his math, history, and civics homework. He just commits anything that he needs to remember to his visual memory. Then, during the tests at school, Brad just closes his eyes and "reads" the material from the pictures in his mind.

Marianne said that she was in the process of transferring Brad to a school that recognizes the different learning styles in children. Most traditional and public schools are based on a left-brain, linear approach to learning, so you may need to do some investigation to find a school that recognizes that ADHD is, in reality, an indication of a right-brain child in a left-brain school.

Like Marianne, you can determine your children's learning style by asking them questions about how they remember and think. Some examples are:

- When you see your children daydreaming, gently ask them to tell you what they're thinking about. Ask whether they're primarily seeing the daydream or whether they're concentrating on thoughts. Daydreams that are vision- or feeling-oriented are indications of right-brain thinking.

- After you and your children see a movie or watch a TV show together, ask them, "What was your favorite part of the show?" Notice, from their answers, whether they paid most attention to how the movie and actors looked (a right-brain thinking style), how the movie made them feel (a right-brain thinking style), the message of the movie (a left-brain thinking style), or what they learned (a left-brain thinking style).

- If you discover that your Indigo Children are right-brained, then it's important to help them develop their natural photographic memory. Be sure to reinforce what a gift they have, and that their visual orientation is a special tool that will help them succeed in many life areas.

ADHD or Creative?

In the book *The Indigo Children,* I wrote about the similarities between gifted and creative children and those who are mislabeled ADHD. I was labeled "gifted" as a child and was put into separate classes, and I skipped ahead one grade. I'm so grateful that the label ADHD didn't exist back then, because I may have been put on medication instead of being enrolled in advanced classes.

These classes fed my soul in a deep, satisfying way. The teachers always had lessons, games, and activities that challenged us to think creatively. We'd conduct word games as a class, which helped us with social skills. I highly recommend having your Indigo Children screened for creativity and gifted characteristics, even if their grades don't reflect this possibility. Many Indigo Children who are bored in normal classrooms show their genius tendencies when they're put into programs geared to their abilities.

Researcher Bonnie Cramond, Ph.D., has extensively studied the similarities between children who are highly creative, and those who are labeled ADHD. Dr. Cramond cites a study of ADHD-diagnosed children where researchers found that half of them scored above the 70th percentile in creativity. And 32 percent of the ADHD-labeled children scored above the 90th percentile for creativity. Unfortunately, very few psychologists and psychiatrists screen for "gifted" criteria when they're conducting evaluations for ADHD or ADD behaviors.

Cramond found scientific research that showed that both groups (highly creative and ADHD) are:

- prone to engage in disruptive, attention-seeking behavior in the classroom.

- not valued by teachers as much as children who are more conforming.

- apt to engage in thrill-seeking or sensation-seeking behaviors. Researchers believe that sensation-seeking may lead a creative person to discover new experiences, which they incorporate into their ideas and inventions. In addition, risk-taking (similar to sensation-seeking) is correlated with business and financial success. This trait may also explain why Indigo Children become easily bored once they "get" what someone is teaching them.

- likely to be "inattentive." They daydream, think of new ideas, and pay attention to inner guidance and spiritual guidance, and tune out conversations or activities that don't ring true or fit with their passion.

- known to exhibit high levels of "overexciteabil-ity," or a tendency to fidget and be hyperactive.

- often passionate and have outbursts of temper.

- frequently socially awkward. They may be shy, defensive, or aloof because they feel different than others, and it's easier to be alone than suffer ridicule.

Dr. Cramond concluded, "Perhaps what differentiates in-dividuals who use their rapid ideation to create versus those who are disruptive and unproductive is the talent and *opportunity* to express their energies and ideas in some cre-ative mode." So, giving your Indigo Children creative out-lets, and giving them support for their "differentness" is essential.

Here's what Indigo Child Dawn says:

Creative expression is really important for expressing your deep feelings. Anytime you can, try drawing or painting something—even if it's just lines. No one will see it but you. Write a poem or a letter to someone you need to talk to. This will help to work through things in life. You need to do something creative every day to release things. Otherwise they will build up and then explode.

❦❦❦ ❦❦❦

✿ *Chapter Eleven* ✿

What Indigo Children Want Us to Know

Most of the books that I reviewed during my research about ADD, ADHD, and learning disabilities featured excellent material by scientists and doctors. Many of these publications were filled with case studies, yet I was surprised by how very few books contained material directly from the children themselves.

Consequently, I decided to include thoughts from the Indigo Children here. I asked my Indigo Child stepdaughter, Nicole, to conduct these interviews. I knew that Indigo Children would share honest feelings from their heart more easily if they were talking with a peer.

Nicole asked Indigo Children of various backgrounds and ages, "What would you like to tell adults that would help us have better relationships with each other?" The Indigo Children welcomed this opportunity to speak and teach. Here are their wise words, which we can all benefit and learn from:

Alec (age 21)

Q: What would you like adults to know so that they can get along better with children?

A: To know that there are things that we young people can do. Adults tend to think that, because of their experience, they know better. It doesn't matter *how long* you've been doing something; it's *what* you've been doing. Not to say all adults are wrong, but they don't always know the way. They should let us learn from our experiences rather from their words. They should let us make decisions because we won't be good at making decisions if they're made for us.

Q: What would you change in the behavior of adults?

A: They should not be so set in their ways. I know a lot of adults who think that this is it. They take for granted the way they feel and do things. They get stuck. They should realize that if they're not happy with something, they can change it. I see a lot of people who are stuck in a job that they don't really like, and they don't take care of themselves, and then they wonder why they don't feel that great. They can take better care of themselves, eat better, and find a job they like. They don't want to change, though, because they've been doing it for so long and it's hard for them to break the pattern. It's habitual. That's what they've been practicing for a long time, and you get really good at what you practice.

Q: What are some values your parents have taught you?

A: Respect for other people's things and other people. To take care of myself. To do my best in what I'm doing and to do what I want to do and do it well.

Q: What is a message you'd like to give adults?

A: Let kids make their own decisions to a certain extent. It doesn't help to punish. Explain to them—don't yell at or spank them. Let them practice making their own decisions because they're the ones who will make their decisions when they're older. If they don't get practice at an early age, they're going to make stupid decisions. I know so many kids whose parents were so strict, and as soon as they got out of the house, they did retarded things, and they hurt themselves because they had no decision-making skills.

Q: What are misconceptions adults create about you?

A: My grandparents don't think I know what's good for me. They really want me to go to school and think that I have to get an education. Times are different, though. They're 70 years old. You don't have to go to a systematic school anymore. People are different now, and it doesn't seem like the school system has changed that much to meet the needs of the people. I don't think you should have to learn about something you aren't interested in. A big part of education is doing what you want to do.

Dawn (age 20)

Q: What do you want adults to know so that it would be easier to get along with them?

A: They need to stop placing so many expectations on kids and let them grow into themselves in a natural way instead of forcing them into a system.

Q: What would you change in the behavior of adults?

A: I think the majority of adults are too money oriented, and it consumes their entire life and they don't pay attention to things that are right in front of them, like their family. Rather than spend time with their family, they would rather go make money, and that's really sad.

Q: What are some misunderstandings adults have about youth?

A: One of the misconceptions is that we are all a lost, wandering generation and we don't have a purpose. I've heard that a lot, and I don't believe it at all. There are some amazing kids out there who are going to be changing this world. It seems that adults are unaware of that. I feel like they think we're lazy and don't have a drive.

Q: How do you think your parents have affected you and who you are now?

A: My parents have taught me so much. They are my best friends in this world. They've taught me a lot of hard lessons, mostly about relationships, because as parents, they were so equally loving and so willing to put in as much energy as it took. Having two forces in my life like that has made me feel like a very complete person. I have so many friends who do not have that relationship with their parents, and I see how they are and their lack of certain things because of it. My parents have been a huge influence in my life. They have basically helped form the beginnings of me. They allowed me to be free with myself.

Q: What do you mean by that?

A: Not many parents will be okay with you not going to college and will not try to force it down your throat and make you do things that they think are good for you instead of what you want to do. I think that was a huge thing—to have that comfort to know that they believed in me so much that they knew I didn't need it, that I could make things happen for myself.

Q: They didn't plan your life?

A: Exactly. I see it so much with one particular friend of mine. She is this wonderful creative artist. She doesn't like dealing with this real-world stuff. Her parents made her go to college, made her graduate and get her degree, because that's what you're supposed to do. And now they're telling her, "You should go get your teaching credential because you need something to fall back on." To me, that is so sad! If I looked at my daughter's paintings and saw that they were that amazing, I would encourage her and completely support her in doing whatever she wanted with it. After all, when you have a passion for something like that, there's no stopping it. It's uncontrollable, and to force yourself to be doing something you don't want to do is unreal to me. I just don't understand at all why you would place that on your children, make them live up to this expectation you put on them. That's why I'm so thankful that my parents never did that to me. It has been very important in my life.

Q: What kinds of expectations do parents put on their kids?

A: I think college is a very big one in my age group and society in general, not just with parents. But I think the parents' pressure comes from society and what the norm is, what everyone is supposed to be doing. "You have to have four years of college and a degree. Then you can get a good job and earn 50 grand and you can drive two hours to work every morning and be unhappy." I don't want to worry about money, but if I don't have a lot, I will try my hardest not to stress about it and just be happy because I'm doing what I want instead of working some job that I have no desire to be at.

Q: Any message you'd like to give adults?

A: Especially for parents, have a very active, conversational relationship with your children. Really try to listen to what they're telling you instead of placing what you think is right onto them. If that were to happen, both people in the relationship would be much happier. This world is so run on money, but don't let it run you. Let your family come before money. To me, your relationships with one another are the most important things in the world; everything else comes second. Your relationship with yourself, your family, and your friends all should take precedence over anything.

Elizabeth (age 16)

Q: What do you want adults to know so that it would be easier to get along with them?

A: Not to be so controlling and let the children learn for themselves.

Q: Why do they need to learn for themselves?

A: It's easier said than done, so if you have the experience yourself, then it has more of an impact on the person instead of being told.

Q: What do you think adults do wrong?

A: Not letting children experience for themselves. Being too judgmental of friends. The first impression is not always the best impression because it doesn't show who the person is. An example is someone who dresses differently, and then judging them based upon looks.

Q: How have your parents affected who you are?

A: I think that they have in every way. That's why it's so important that parents know certain things about their kids. Parents are the people who the kids are with all the time, so it's very important that they're open with them. Honest with them.

And not pressing opinions too much, but also teaching very important values. Some important values are friendship and trust and responsibility. It's important that they show their kids by way of example, and not just by telling.

Q: Any message you'd like to give adults?

A: If I could, I would have them switch places so they could see how it is to be a child, because it seems like they forget. When punishing you or not letting you do certain things, it seems like they don't remember how much it affected them when their parents did it to them.

Adam (age 14)

Q: What would you like adults to know so that it would be easier to get along with kids your age?

A: That they're not always right. I think adults are opinionated, and they'll back it up and they're stubborn, and even if they do think you're right, in the end they won't admit it because you're like a third of their age.

Q: Why won't they admit they're wrong?

A: I wouldn't want to admit that a three-year-old's right—that's probably what it seems like to them.

Q: How would it help if they did admit when they were wrong?

A: It would be easier to talk to them.

Q: What are misconceptions adults create about your age group?

A: That we're out of control, crazy, kind of stupid, I guess, like we'll do anything. That's unfair to stereotype people like that. In some cases, it's true, but you can't stereotype someone, because half of them are that, and the other half aren't. I know they are a lot crazier compared to other people, and if you scale it against an adult, that's unfair, because the adults have been living a lot longer and know a lot more.

Q: Any message you'd like to give adults?

A: To respect us, and not stereotype teenagers or kids as being inferior.

Q: Why do you think they think teens are inferior?

A: It seems like adults think they know the answers, and most of the time I've just followed it, and now I've come to question it more—just systems as a whole—and I can find flaws in them. I know those won't change. Like the school system. I don't like it. I'd rather hear what the students are thinking than listen to some guy lecture. Discussions would be a lot better. You're going to learn from your peers later on in life, and the teacher could be part of the discussion, but I'm sick of listening to a teacher all day, every day.

Q: Do you learn from that?

A: Yeah, but all it is, is regurgitating the knowledge I've already learned, and that's pointless. It's easy to get an *A* on a test, because all you have to do is remember what he said, and that isn't difficult. I also think that they put you down for making mistakes, but mistakes are the best way to learn.

Q: What would you suggest they do instead?

A: I think everyone should sit around a table and have a discussion on the topic we're learning about, instead of listening to someone lecture. I know kids who fall asleep, and I feel like falling asleep in some of my classes. And it's possible to hide out in the back of a class, which is what I like to do, because it's kind of boring. If you're having a discussion, you're all looking at each other, and you have to be part of it, and you can't just go in the back and fade out.

Q: What would you change in the behavior of adults?

A: To be more accepting to kids growing up, because right now our world is in a transition from industrial to technology. You can see that with all these 20-year-olds making millions of dollars. I think that some parents are learning from their kids about computers, and I think that the new generation knows more about that, and if the old generation doesn't let us teach them, they're going to get caught behind.

Chris (age 20)

Q: What do you want adults to know so that it would be easier for you to get along with them?

A: I would like them to not take life so seriously. They should have more fun.

Q: Are there any messages that you would like to give adults so that you could get along with them better?

A: To take care of their bodies and to do as much yoga as possible.

Q: Are there any misconceptions that adults have about you and other people your age?

A: That we don't know what we're talking about. But we know a lot more than people think. It does seem that adults are becoming more and more open, though, and that's a good thing.

David (age 21)

Q: What do you want adults to know so that you can get along with them better?

A: Personally, I have no problem with adults. But I think that there's a problem in general with the way adults "hold the hands" of their children, and the way that they protect the children by not allowing them to explore things for themselves. That's the way that you learn the best. That's the way I learned a lot of things—by figuring it out for myself. If you have someone holding your hand the whole way, then you can't learn it as well.

Nicole (age 21)

Q: What do you want adults to know so that it would be easier to get along with them?

A: For them to get along better with me, I think that they would first have to get rid of prejudgments about my age. Instead of looking at me as a 21-year-old who doesn't know anything, which is what they tend to do, they should look at me as a human being. And be open to, maybe even learning from me instead of being shut off because I'm young and supposedly don't know anything.

Q: If you could, what might you change in the behavior of adults?

A: I would like to see them be more open to change. If they're not feeling good, to not just blame it on their age. "Oh, wait until you get to be my age." I hear that so much. Here they are, 50 years old, and it sounds like they're ready to die, like there's no turning back.

Also, I wish adults would be more open to learning. When they get to a certain age, it seems like adults think that they're done learning. Mainly, what I'd like to see change is their closed-minded attitudes.

Q: How have your parents affected who you are?

A: They've definitely affected who I am. The biggest thing that I would like to thank them for is the freedom that they've given me. They've allowed me to be who I want to be, and that has made me like them. It's made me not want to rebel against them, and it's made me enjoy their companionship. I'll see behavior in my mom, and then I'll see myself doing the same thing. And with my dad, I know I'm so similar to him. I hope that parents realize how much their kids are going to be like them. But kids are smarter than adults think. Kids are not going to be how their parents *tell* them to be; they're going to be the way their parents *act*.

Q: Are there any messages that you would like to give adults?

A: Give the kids freedom. Don't let them hurt themselves, but don't be too controlling, because you can't control a human being. Never tell your children, "If it wasn't for me, you wouldn't be here." You *chose* to have the children, so you should treat them like the wonderful creations that they are. Pay more attention to your kids. Every person that I know that is high-strung and sometimes annoying to be around is that way because their parents did not pay attention to them. They want more attention. And then I'll see other people whose parents gave them so much love and attention and always made them feel wanted, and they're more mellow and seem to flow through life.

Adults, don't forget your childhood. Don't forget all the things that you did when you were young. Even though you may be done with it now, your kids still have to go through it. It's just a process in life. If you take away the availability of experiences from your kids, then you're basically taking away their childhood, and then they'll have to go through it later.

I have a friend who was raised a devout Jehovah's Witness — they don't celebrate birthdays or Christmas or anything like that. His parents were very strict. He has now moved away, and he's going crazy. He parties all the time and does tons of drugs because he couldn't experience these things under a safe roof. I think it's so important to not try to control people. Just let a person be who they are.

Ryan (age 20)

Q: What would you change in the behavior of adults?

A: I don't know if they do it on purpose, but adults seem like they don't know how to relate to young people. The way they act is unapproachable, where they won't understand or they'll tell you what's right or wrong about whatever you're talking about. A lot of times when I was younger, I felt like adults didn't know what I was talking about. Almost every time I came into contact with most adults, they would try to give me advice as to what's right and wrong. They're so quick to give solutions that it's almost unreal. It's not authentic, either; it's like they're saying things that they've said before, or that they think they're supposed to say. I wish they'd come from their truth and hearts instead of their heads. Adults lie a lot, too.

Q: Why do you think they lie?

A: A lot of times, adults don't think you're ready for certain information, or they don't want to be completely honest because they don't think you'll understand it, or they've read books about how to deal with these situations. I know that they try their hardest, but for some reason, it doesn't work.

Q: If adults were more honest, would it help you?

A: Definitely. Especially if they're more open about things when their kids are at a younger age. If adults were more honest, it would make things a lot easier.

Q: What are misconceptions adults have about you or young people in general?

A: For a long time, it was about how I looked. I admit that I was a crazy little man for a while, but the fact that they'll look at that and not be nice to you because of it, not give you a chance. That's sad.

Q: How would you have preferred to be treated, and would that have made you act any differently?

A: Probably not. I did it on purpose to an extent. It gets you attention, and I kind of liked that people thought that about me. Oh, this guy is trouble. Looking back, it was because of the attention I got from people. The looks I got from people. And now I don't want that attention that's brought about by the way I look.

Q: What has changed?

A: I don't know. I used to have my face pierced. I got to the point where I hated people looking at me. I couldn't stand it. Maybe it's just growing up, growing out of a phase.

Q: Is there any message you'd like to give adults?

A: I think a lot of adults lose touch with their younger self as they grow older, and they lose contact with the younger generation. They aren't around them. And as time changes, kids go through a lot of different stuff. A lot of it's different, but a lot is the same. Kids all go through the same stuff—it's just a different time. Adults forget what it was like; they forget how to relate to younger people.

If they can find that youthful part of themselves somehow, they will feel more whole. They will realize that youthful part of them again, because you never really lose it. It's not like you grow out of it, you just lose sight of it because of all the responsibilities, and growing up. So many people lose sight of it that they have a hard time relating to a younger generation because they don't know it anymore; they don't live it. They need to not lose sight of it.

They get so stuck in their ways of being a grown-up that they forget what it's like to have fun. I see it in so many people. Try not to forget the way a child thinks. Kids don't pass judgment on people.

Charles (age 22)

Q: What do you want adults to know about Indigo Children?

A: The Indigos are probably the most misunderstood members of our society. In a fast-paced "on-the-go-every-minute" society, adults don't have the time to answer the endless questions or give the 100 percent attention that the Indigos need. So, Indigo Children, in turn, become labeled as "nuisances."

Obviously, the Indigos were built with the potential to become smarter and stronger than the average adult. So one must assume that they're here to serve a greater purpose. And believe me, they're no accident (although that's what the conception may have been—but that's another story).

Q: Why do you think that adults and children sometimes don't get along with each other?

A: I don't just think, I *know* exactly why parents and children don't get along these days. Parents feel that the children are out of control, and the children feel like their parents could never understand them in a million years. You know what? They're both right. Indigos *are* out of control. But that's the beauty of it.

See, you walk down the street and talk to people, and all you hear is complaints. About what, you ask? Well, I think you know—government seems to be number one. Closely followed by money, domestic issues, etc. I hear it all day long, too, but who is going to do anything about it? You? I didn't think so.

Right now we're all forced to be so imbedded into our lives and goals that even though we know things could be a lot better in our world, we settle and say, "I guess it could be worse." But fret not, our saviors are here. If you can't control your children, do you think the government can?

Q: If you could have every parent of an Indigo Children in one room and could only say a few sentences to them, what would you say?

A: I would tell them, "I would never expect you to understand us, or think our actions are tolerable. We are here for a great purpose, and although you cannot see any beneficial uses for our tendencies, you soon will. Although none of you want to think about it or admit it, you're raising warriors. And I don't mean that in the "hand-to-hand-fight-to-the-death" sense.

Q: What do you think the purpose of Indigo Children is?

A: Fifteen to twenty years from now, when the Indigos are contributing members of our society, something wonderful will happen. They will grow more and more fed up with our overbearing government by the day. Just imagine a society full of people just like your children. Sounds almost scary, doesn't it? These children will have the same adverse reaction to authority their whole lives.

When you label them ADD or ADHD and give them chemicals like Ritalin or Imipramine or Dizipramine, all you do is temporarily restrain their actions. It's not the children's fault that they were born this way. You and the Indigo Children can coexist peacefully. But to do so, you absolutely have to loosen your grip of authority. I don't mean to let the children do whatever they want by any means. You just have to realize that your children are programmed to rebel. The harder you chain them up, the more they will rebel.

Q: Since you're an Indigo Child, what advice would you give to parents or teachers of Indigo Children?

A: Indigo Children can smell a lie from a mile away. They can also sense when someone is upset or has bad intentions. So maybe your best bet is to just relax. Nobody said having a child was easy, and your children *will* calm down—eventually. When you talk to your children, show that you're being genuine. Look them in the eye; don't make threats or false promises. Explain to them how their actions make you feel and how they affect you. Don't tell them they're screwing their lives up or anything. Just remember it like this—negative input, negative output; positive input, positive output.

Hunter (age 21)

Q: What would you like adults to know so that it would be easier to get along with them?

A: While we might not know things that they know based upon the fact that we're younger than they are, we know tons of things they don't know based upon the virtue of our youth.

Q: What would you change in the behavior of adults?

A: The tendency to make assumptions and generalizations based upon incorrect information.

Q: Is there anything you'd like to say to adults?

A: Try to drop predisposed ideas of what you think I mean when I'm saying something. Just relax, too, because 99 percent of the people on this earth end up having an okay life. Don't try to force things with your kids. They're going to grow if they're going to grow. You can only give them a place to sleep, and food to eat, and your love. We'll figure out what we want to do as we experience it. When you put pressure on us and try to fit us in to what you want us to be, it's hard to do that simply because the parent wants to impress another adult at a dinner party. Someone tells you what their kid is doing, so you want to tell them what your kid is doing. The fact of the matter is that nobody really knows what they want when they're 18 years old.

❦❦❦ ❦❦❦

❧ Chapter Twelve ❧

Astrology and the Indigo Children

As I mentioned in Chapter 3, we can remember part of our personal Life Purpose by looking at the characteristics of our sun sign. Although it's simplistic to only focus on the sun sign, this basic element still provides us with a wealth of insight.

Similarly, you can understand your Indigo Children by studying what their sun sign reveals. Astrologer Michele Avanti has done astrological charts for children and their families for many years. In this chapter, she offers us some insights about how best to work, talk, and play with Indigo Children, according to their sun signs. Of course, to gain an even richer understanding of your Indigo Children, you may want to get their entire astrological chart done. (In fact, Michele can make charts for you and your Indigo Children. Her contact information is in the Resources section of this book.) By getting an astrological chart done, you can learn about the various planets and aspects affecting your children's personality, behavior, and Life Purpose.

An Introduction to Astrology

The stars have been studied for at least 4,000 years. According to ancient records, the Babylonians studied the stars for patterns and then correlated these patterns to mundane events. These geometric patterns were later termed *Ptolemaic* after Ptolemy, who was an avid astrologer and astronomer in his day.

As astrologers watched these planets traveling through the constellations, they noted that each constellation had a particular effect on the planet. Thus, they developed an understanding of the influence not only of each planet, but of each constellation as well—and also the effects of the planets as they combined in geometric patterns in the sky. (These patterns are called *aspects* by current-day astrologers.)

In the 20th century, we came to understand the meaning of resonance. This is the response of one body to another body through sound, magnetics, electronics, microwaves, and so on. Prior to the 20th century, any actions that resulted from a resonant response would not have been understood and would have been considered magic.

During the 21st century, I believe, resonance will vindicate the study and use of astrology from magic or a so-called pseudo-science. We will learn that each of the bodies in our solar system leaves an electromagnetic imprint on human DNA at the exact moment that a child takes its first breath (actually, when any Earth creature takes its first breath). So, as these celestial bodies move through space and make a geometric pattern to their imprint on personal DNA, we get a resonant response. I believe this is how astrology works!

For parents of Indigo Children:

• Understanding the nature of your children at the outset is going to be extremely helpful, and this is where astrology is meaningful. From the moment a child is born, astrologically, we have the information that will give us a toolbox for helping expedite the growth and learning of each child.

• With just the date of birth of your children and the birthdays of each family member, you can get the planetary positions you need to understand their basic nature. First, let's look at the elements and how they relate to your Indigo Children.

The Elements

The first element is Fire.
It's the element of creativity.

Fire is an active, creative element. Fire does not sit still very well, does it? It's constantly flickering and moving, and given the opportunity to run wild, it can burn through an entire house or thousands of acres of land. When contained properly (disciplined) it can provide warmth, light, and the ability to cook food; thus, it can help sustain life when it's properly controlled.

Children who have a preponderance of Fire in their charts will be very active. They can even be hyperactive. They don't like to sit still. They prefer to be the center of attention. They're very creative and dramatic, and frequently can be called inspired. These children will have a need to be doing things. The way we can best work with these children is to give them things that will keep them active, inspired, and creative. This will satisfy their nature.

To ask Fire children to sit still for a long period of time in silence would be an enormous challenge for them and would offer no obvious benefit. However, if you need to have them sit still for a long time, give them some creative work that challenges their particular level of consciousness. Then they'll be able to work with you.

The Fire signs are: *Aries, Leo, and Sagittarius.*

The second element is Earth.
It's an element of physical materiality.

Earth is very stable. When you look at a pile of earth or a mountain of earth, you don't see anything active. Rather, you see something calm and secure, with the strength and ability to offer sustenance. When it's organized through human efforts, it can become beautiful and flourish, as in a park or garden. Earth provides a food supply when it's seeded, watered, and given time to grow. If overseeded, some seeds will not grow, while the stronger ones will strangle others. If overwatered, the seeds die because the earth becomes like mud and cannot hold the roots of the seeds. If underwatered, it dries up, becomes hard, and cracks without giving life to the plants. If you do not give it enough time, the plants will not mature, and they won't flower or give fruit.

In many ways, this describes Earth people. Earth individuals do not move quickly. They think deeply and have a need to feel secure. They want to own things because there's security in ownership. They're loyal and dependable, and it's against their nature to suddenly uproot and move. Like the earth itself, these individuals can be seeded with ideas or direction and then nurtured with love and encouragement. Then you need to step back and give them the time they need to grow. If you give them too many ideas or too much direction, they become overwhelmed and cannot produce anything well. If you baby them with too much nurturing, they become dependent and will not take root to stand on their own. If you undernurture them, they become hard and lifeless, and it will take more of your attention (fertilizer) to soften them, as well as more love (water) to bring them back to life. Earth people will take their time to do a job well. They are persistent like the earth itself; they seldom give up.

Children with a preponderance of Earth in their charts need to be given boundaries to feel loved and secure. They should not be pushed but rather, led; they should not be uprooted without being given ample time to accept the situation, and if they experience sudden changes, they should be given opportunities to express themselves in a physical way. When angry, these children should be given a safe means of expressing themselves physically. They may choose to dance, jump rope, throw a ball, or run with a dog or mold clay. Discipline is a sign of love to them. They need it to feel secure. Give them rules, and if they ask, then tell them why. Offer them encouragement and time to work through new ideas or difficult issues.

The Earth signs are: *Taurus, Virgo, and Capricorn.*

The third element is Air.
It's the element of mental activity.

Air is a very changeable kind of element. It can go from hot to cold; it can move, and it can even change form. Air can move between gas and vapor. It can be clear or foggy. It's hard to capture and hold. It's seldom still, but sometimes silent. At other times, it can crackle with electricity or snap with terrifying thunder.

Humans cannot communicate without the power of breath—thus, air. It is air that sustains the soprano's note, and air that whispers on the stage. Without air, we would not live, think, or communicate. Air carries the oxygen to our hearts and gives us a signal of life when we're born. Oxygen in the air feeds our brains and gives us the power to think and understand.

Children who are predominantly Air are thinkers. They're talkative, filled with ideas and creative thought-provoking energy. They will debate in whispers or loud, sudden, dramatically direct responses. Seldom are they silent for very long. They will want to understand what is being said and won't necessarily respond to "Do it this way!" types of commands. Unlike the Earth children, Air children don't want rules unless they understand them, and even then they might feel a need to change them. One should take the time to fully explain the what, how, and why of anything related to Air children. Give them time for questions, and then allow the children to begin the project. Expect lots of questions, and give these kids the opportunity to explore the answers. Let them join you in setting the rules or types of discipline that will bind them. These things will give them both the challenges and the confidence they need to grow.

The Air signs are: *Gemini, Libra, and Aquarius.*

The fourth element is Water.

It's the element of emotions.

The moon moves the tides, and since humans are predominantly made of water, the moon also moves us. Full moons can bring out romantic, psychic, sensitive, passionate, and angry characteristics. Water, when given parameters, responds in different yet consistent ways. Focused, as in a brook running to the sea, water is bubbling and joyful. Placed in a container, water is silent and placid. Forced from the earth by internal pressures, it's dramatic and beautiful, rising into the air as geysers. Pushed to its limits over a rock-laden cliff, it becomes the waterfall—thunderous, loud, and dramatic. Finally, when it's placed in a cold environment, it becomes silent, frozen, solid, and immobile.

Children who are predominantly Water will show all of these characteristics. They're very sensitive to the feelings of everyone around them. Given safe parameters, they're placid. Given internal turmoil, they become dramatically reactive and may spout and explode with fury. Pushed to their limits, they will dramatically crash through barriers with more power than you'd expect. Finally, placed in an environment without the warmth and love they need, they may become despondent and recoil from the world at large.

Water children need to be nurtured and loved. They should be encouraged to express their feelings and trust themselves. Their sensitive nature requires tactile experiences, and they should be encouraged to create with their hands and to express themselves with their bodies. They need more hugs than Fire or Air, and even a little more than Earth children.

The Water signs are: *Cancer, Scorpio, and Pisces.*

How the Elements Work Together

Fire is fed by Air. Earth is fed by Water. Fire scorches Earth. Air travels around the Earth. Air does not mix with Water. Water puts out Fire. Earth puts out Fire. Water cannot dominate air. Earth can smother Air.

So if we're to help our children work together, we need to know the predominant elements in their charts. Asking a Fire child to work with a Water child , or worse yet, a Water teacher, could have some disastrous outcomes. When we understand the nature of our children and ourselves, we're better equipped to honor and fulfill the needs of both.

A Look at the Signs

Now, Michele Avanti gives you a simple outline of the nature of each sign. Please note that a child who has their sun or moon in any of these signs, or a preponderance of planets and sensitive points in any of these signs, will have more of these characteristics. This should help you better understand their needs.

Aries
(March 20–April 21)

Aries children love to create big, eye-catching, award-winning projects that put them out in front. These children are highly active and physical. They need to be seen and acknowledged for their accomplishments. They're award-oriented individuals and thrive on prizes.

Their bodies are important to them, and they love to show them off. These children tend to be athletic, competitive, and physical, and they can be aggressive—even explosive when angry. Give them physical projects if you want silence, and tell them that there will be rewards for concentration as well as endurance. They're not necessarily good at discipline unless it's a physical or athletic situation resulting in recognition. Wardrobe is also important to them. They express themselves through their clothing and sometimes will express their love for you through it as well.

Health issues for Aries surround the head. The saying "big head" was coined for Aries, and it tells the story well. Teach these children humility. When you understand that we're all equal but have different states of consciousness, then the children will realize that competition relates only to the lower worlds. Some days they'll win and sometimes they'll lose, but there's no loss to the soul because we always gain when we experience life! This is the key to health for Aries.

Taurus
(April 21–May 20)

Taurus children can be the most stubborn of all. Imagine a mountain. It takes dynamite to move it. That's the equivalent of a person with a preponderance of Taurus in their chart. These children love the security of routine and will be loyal to a fault. They need to be taught how to let go and let God. *Change* is a negative word to them, and they need to befriend it.

Start teaching them the cycles of life as soon as they're born, and keep teaching this. Help them celebrate the change of seasons so that they learn to focus their attention on what is coming instead of what has been. Encourage them to enjoy and then give away some of their things, instead of hoarding them. It can be very valuable for these kids to take part in a program such as "Toys for Tots" at Christmastime.

Taureans also need to expand their way of looking at the world and to recognize their own shortcomings so that they'll learn how to get the help they need when they hit a road-block. Discipline through routine comes easy for them, while anything new seems very difficult at first. Instigate a monthly schedule of exploring options that will help them expand. Remember that they're stubborn, so encourage them to develop the program. This is how it becomes their idea and not yours. They love rituals.

They may be the most tactile of all the signs, and Taurus is very sensitive to the softness and comfort of their linens and clothing. Also, anything that makes them feel important can be used to help them break through fears. Encourage them with praise, and since they love photographs of themselves, take a picture of their accomplishments. They also love sweets, but I don't recommend ever using them for rewards with these children. Sweets can be very detrimental to their health and become a crutch for them later in life if situations challenge their self-worth. Being very kinesthetic, Taureans tend to indulge themselves with food and drink and may develop weight issues. Rewards for the Taureans should be luxury items, photographs, and anything that pampers the body.

Health issues for Taureans relate to the throat. Self-expression is more important than security and luxury. This is the key to health for a Taurus. Teach your children to speak despite their fear of losing something. Remind them that their angels will help them form the words even when they're terrified of losing something precious to them.

Gemini
(May 21–June 20)

Gemini means ideas, ideas, and more ideas. Their minds are an ever-changing pallette of ideas. These individuals are so busy with their ideas that it's difficult for them to focus. They talk, talk, talk, and you wonder when they have the time to think; but in actuality, they never stop thinking.

They can have difficulty sleeping at night because their mind just keeps going. You will need to start teaching these children early in life to relax and calm their minds. Active meditation is recommended. Teaching Geminis to work on answering their own questions is also recommended. They need to realize that they're actually connected to a higher power and have the answers.

These are very wiry, active children. They're not necessarily interested in sports, but are interested in music, and this can be their greatest asset. Through a choice of music, and encouragement in this area, you may help your Gemini kids relax and focus. They also love parties and social gatherings of all kinds. These can be rewards for focusing on and completing a project. They're learning about choices in this life, and they need to understand that their attitude is key.

Health issues for Geminis involve the arms and lungs. The breath is life itself. This is their key to health. Gemini must say and do what is aligned with their thoughts. The arms point to the direction we see and the words we speak, and they're formed from the breath we take. So teach them to speak, point, and act on what they say, and that will keep Geminis healthy.

Cancer
(June 21–July 20)

Cancer makes for a sensitive, moody, and family-oriented nature. These individuals will be driven more often by their feelings than their mind. They have a tenacious attitude and are extremely protective of anyone they consider family. They want to nurture and be nurtured. They love food, home life, ancestry, antiques, and the history of their family or nation. They are the patriots of their homeland.

As children, they need to be given space to work through their feelings. They see issues on a large scale and look at situations through the reactions of their family, ancestry, and nation. They have a difficult time dealing with criticism, so it's imperative that they're taught early on how to work through issues without personalizing them or feeling threatened by being evaluated.

Their sensitive natures need to be considered whenever they're being taught. Reactions of these individuals will be to draw back inside themselves or clam up, yet they have a hard time letting go. Issues and criticism stay with them long after the teacher considers it done. It's best to give them the task of reviewing their own shortcomings and then work with them to see more realistically.

Cancers must learn to release feelings and let go of situations that are old. Help them to use the past but focus on the present while activating their future with long-term goals. Teach flexibility in all things. Much can be done through home projects, including cooking for both males and females. Water has a calming influence on these individuals. They would enjoy swimming lessons. To help them relax, consider giving them a fountain for their room or a CD of water music.

Health issues for Cancers surround the stomach and digestive processes. They should never be made to eat when they're upset; it can cause sickness and obesity. The digestive process is one of taking in nourishment and slowly working it into the system so that it can feed all parts of the body. The key to health for Cancers is to nourish themselves by taking in the love that is given (that means learning to love themselves first). Then, through the process of examining, filtering, and releasing, they can return it to others. For Cancers, health is directly connected to the nurturing of self and then others—not the other way around.

Leo
(July 21–August 20)

Leos are leaders, and they need more attention than any other sign. Much like a fire in the fireplace needs to be stoked, watched, and continually fed with air and wood, Leo children want to be seen in and applauded for everything they do. They need your praise—it's like the wood that keeps a fire secure. They also need your ideas or direction. This is like the air that fire needs to grow.

These children are creative, social, fun-loving, and enjoy being the center of attention. If they're not given creative challenges and praise, they may use negative behavior to catch your attention. Their nature is like that of a child and therefore, they can indulge themselves in irresponsible behavior. If this is overlooked instead of corrected, it will become a pattern of self-sabotage in their adult lives.

Find creative challenges for these children. Acting classes, dancing, singing, comedies, and social clubs that include any of the arts are all good choices. If these kids start down the road of negative behavior, you can quickly correct this by letting them work with less capable or handicapped children. Leo individuals love children and want to entertain. Give them opportunities to do so. Acting, puppet shows, magic tricks or entertaining at another children's parties can give the Leo an opportunity to be seen and to lead, which is what their heart desires.

Health issues connect to the heart and the back for Leos. The key is to encourage them to follow their heart and rest between experiences. They must be taught early on how not to burn out, but rather how to smolder as a good fire does, keeping us all warm and content.

Virgo
(August 21–September 20)

Virgos are very serious children. Laughter is not easily understood with this nature, and everything must be justified. The Virgo child is practical, hard-working, and service oriented. Helping these children have fun is necessary to give them a rounded life. They feel best when serving others, but they should be taught early on that a balanced life includes time to rest and enjoy themselves.

Rest is not part of the mind of the Virgo-dominant individual. Their minds are constantly analyzing, and too frequently they fall into self-criticism. Teach them that we're equal and that although each individual differs in consciousness while on this Earth plane, we are not to judge anyone. Instead, they should simply acknowledge others as souls, and know that each one has their own Divine plan . . . all of which is in perfect harmony at every moment in time.

Virgos are capable of treading a long, persistent journey and meeting changes first with their mind and then through practical assessment, slowly making change. These children need to be taught to speak honestly about their feelings without criticizing others. The key is to teach them that what annoys us the most in another is a reflection of our own fears. Sometimes it's from a past-life event, and sometimes from something in the present. Help them to release deep-seated emotions with laughter. Hypochondria can be a challenge for Virgos if they don't learn to properly focus their minds on important issues. Putting thoughts on paper can be helpful.

Health issues for Virgos surround the colon, and possible impaction. This is the result of hanging on to resentments that have not been aired or expressed out loud.

Libra
(September 21–October 20)

Big ideas and grand conversation is the foundation for Libra. Asking these children to be silent can be a difficult request, especially if they're seated next to a Gemini. Libra minds constantly consider relationships and social venues. They want to know how to fit in and relate to others. Beauty is very important to them. Holding their attention requires beautiful words and stories about people. Libra wants to know how people socialize and communicate in harmony.

Libras love to talk, and they tend to avoid physical exercise. They may appear lazy to the rest of us. How do you get Libras to take action? Promise them a good story about people. This is also how to teach them history or any other subject. Create details that involve people and their relationships with love, war, family, country, and animals. These children love socializing and dressing up. This can be the type of reward that gets them to work. My nephew is a Libra, and he would always help me out if I promised to sit with him and talk about things that interested him.

You'll be surprised by the depth of thoughts these children have. They think in big terms. When my nephew Matt was just four years old, he discussed the courage of bees with me. That is the incredible mind of a Libra.

Libras' greatest challenge is being true to themselves and disallowing any fear they may have about fitting into society. They want to be accepted and to be one of the beautiful people. This desire is so strong that they may fall under the spell of peer pressure and succumb to substance abuse of various kinds. So it's imperative that as a parent of a Libra child, you create an environment conducive to the acceptance, appreciation, and encouragement of individuality.

From the moment you begin working with Libra children, you need to help them build self-esteem based on personally designed standards, instead of competition with others. Explain how you developed *your* standards of integrity and how you developed your self-esteem. Encourage the Libra children to follow through with their deepest feelings, and applaud them when they do. Help them to choose famous people or saints to emulate.

The health issues of Libras involve the gall bladder, which produces bile that helps in the digestion of fats. Fats are likened to the satisfying parts of life, the excesses and the like. Much like whipped cream's beautiful appearance belies its lack of sustenance, the Libra needs to realize that the so-called beautiful people and the "good life" they lead is nothing more than whipped cream—tantalizing but without sustenance. The Libra individual needs to remove the illusion of beauty and become truthful in words and actions. This is Libra's key to health.

Scorpio
(October 21–November 20)

The Scorpio's waters run deep. Scorpio is deeply emotional, seated in issues of power, secrets, silence, sexuality, and the occult. What is hidden from sight, conversation, or social acceptance is of considerable interest to the Scorpio mind. Here you have a child who desires to know the secrets of the universe and all that goes on behind closed doors. Scorpio children are intensely passionate, silently probing, and secretly desire to *know* so that they can gain control in every area of their lives. They're very psychic and read the emotions of others like a newspaper. Parents of Scorpio children must realize the depth of their character and steer them to use their detective talents to enhance humankind instead of falling prey to selfish choices.

These children are transformers. They transform others through their intense reach into the darker parts of human beings. Like surgeons, they bring the most intimate issues to light. Scorpio children have the ability to shock and terrify their teachers with their revelations and blunt questions. Awareness of this characteristic can help a teacher or parent avoid being shocked. Instead, encourage the children to pursue answers to their own questions through books or interviews with professionals in appropriate fields.

When working with Scorpio children, parents must recognize the depth of their questioning minds. They should be encouraged to question, but also be taught that the law of noninterference is the first of all the laws. Interfering with another's state of consciousness just for the shock value brings about karmic consequences (which means more tests), not the power they seek. If you teach these children that true power resides within them and not in controlling others, you will have taken them a step closer to the angels they are.

Scorpio children need to be taught to express the depth of their feelings without blaming others for their woes. They need to see from a very early age that everything in their universe is the result of their choices, either in the here-and-now or due to agreements made before incarnating.

You can help Scorpios understand other people's perspectives and motives by mentally playing detective with respect to people's spiritual natures. In any social interaction, teach Scorpio children to focus on the clues: to this person's mission in life, or to this person's key lesson, or to what this person is really trying to achieve. This can assist them in making choices that will enhance their understanding of real power.

Health issues for the Scorpio individual revolve around the reproductive organs. The secret of creation is at the seat of power. The key to health for these individuals is to come to terms with their own immortality and their power of creation, which first requires recognition of one's responsibility in every choice made. Make sure you teach them that everything they do—thought, word, and action—is based on their power to choose. This is their power of creation. We create everything in our universe through choice.

Always teach Scorpio children to choose to keep their power and not give it away. Whenever we say: "He made me do this, or I had to do that," we've given our power away. Scorpio individuals must learn early on to choose in all things, thus keeping their power and remaining healthy.

Sagittarius
(November 21–December 20)

Sagittarian children are creative and will want to explore everything. They tend to be fearless and will walk to the edge of the cliff to see what's below. They get bored with sticking to one subject or repeating the same thing over again. They are quick, and want to be challenged with new ideas, new horizons, and a fast-paced environment. They're naturally drawn to learning and need little encouragement to succeed.

Teach your Sagittarius child to focus on something long enough to master it before beginning another project. Early on, encourage Sagittarian kids to keep a life journal, whether written, on tape, on video, or digital. A journal enhances their ability to focus. Tell them that giving rewards for completing projects is more important than the project's value.

Teaching that time is relevant—to both the growth of giant trees and also corporations—is also essential. Simple projects like growing even one plant from a seed can help the Sagittarius individual value prudence, discipline, and time.

Also, much can be taught and learned during travel. These children spread their wings in foreign lands, libraries, bookstores, movie theaters, and on the Internet. They enjoy stretching the family's horizons and may surprise you with the companions they bring home for dinner.

Sagittarians want to travel beyond the state of consciousness of the family. Given the chance, they will challenge their parents' minds by what they achieve. These children want to know more about God and the angels than most children. They want to understand how to travel in God's realm as well as on Earth. So give them a fertile ground to explore all of God's possibilities. They may want to go to lectures you would never consider attending. Go with them, and you'll find that these children will expand your mind as they reach for the stars.

Whatever you do with Sagittarius children, don't fence them in. The entire universe is theirs to explore, and you'll lose them if you place boundaries around their learning. Give them the tools to make practical choices without limiting their reach by your own fears. Sagittarius children are eternally optimistic, so know this and help them with practical tools to achieve their dreams.

Health issues for Sagittarians surround the thighs. Travel for these individuals is usually blessed, but they must be taught to keep their hunger to know and explore in balance with their need for rest. This will protect them from burning out and will keep them healthy.

Capricorn
(December 21–January 20)

Capricorns are a combination of farsighted vision and the persistence to achieve it. These children are practical and ambitious. They set their minds on big goals and then employ practical steps to achieve them. They're not good at just relaxing and having fun. They know exactly what to do in a tough situation.

They can control their emotions better than any other zodiac sign and thus can keep their heads in a crisis situation. Capricorn children should be taught to express their feelings so that others realize what they're experiencing. Their poker faces can keep a parent guessing. This can be an asset in a big business negotiation later in life but will create a void in their emotional nature if the parents personalize those blank looks and avoid giving the children the nurturing they need.

Capricorn children appear to have it all under control, but they really desire discipline and practical boundaries in order to feel loved. They need to be taught to nurture, and to understand what makes them feel nurtured. Security, caution, prudence, and a conservative attitude are the nature of Capricorns. They will be good in math and in any meticulous skill. However, they prefer to handle the details with others, rather than all by themselves. They make great administrators.

A very valuable gift you can give Capricorn children would be to teach them how to keep each day of their lives in balance. Explain that we are made up of physical, emotional, mental and spiritual parts, and that each part needs nourishment each day. At the end of each day, let them recount how they've nurtured each part of themselves.

Also, a parent needs to recognize the child's proclivity for stress. These children express stress differently from most. They remain silent and look totally in control even when they're stressed out. Teach them that laughter is the key to managing such situations. At a very early age, you can teach them to incorporate other good stress-releasing skills as well.

A simple technique is to take a deep breath, hold it for a few seconds, then repeat this two more times and conclude by their thinking of the funniest thing they can and start laughing out loud. When we were children, we used to look at each other and run an index finger across our lips making a blubb . . . blubb . . . blubb . . . blubb sound that looks quite ridiculous and would make the teary-eyed one start laughing. A parent or teacher must be willing to risk looking ridiculous to teach Capricorns to let go and laugh.

Health issues for the Capricorn individual involve the knees. This relates to their ability to be flexible. We kneel with our knees, and Capricorn needs to learn to kneel and ask for help instead of trying to take it all on their shoulders. We know Capricorns are tough, but if they want to stay healthy, they need to remember that we all need someone to lean on from time to time.

Aquarius
(January 21–February 20)

Aquarian individuals carry their own soapbox with them at all times. They are orators of the planet, speaking for the good of the whole, pushing us into a more progressive society. Aquarius is the sign of revolution, progress, universal brotherhood, friendship, and inventive genius.

Aquarius children seek to understand what you have to say, and it had better be logical if you are to satisfy these kids. They want knowledge and will immediately apply it to their foundation of logic. These children love to think and talk.

Aquarian children don't see things as they are, but rather in light of their usefulness. This may annoy you if you're a practical, socially directed parent. For example, Aquarian-dominant children may use your best towel to dry the family dog. They may rewire your kitchen appliances so that they work in tandem, and use parts of your hair dryer to achieve this result. Will you be happy about all this? Well, if you perceive it as wreaking havoc in your life, the answer is no. But this is not the best response you could give Aquarian kids. They have a driving desire to know *how* things work and will logically toil on things to find their answers.

Guide these inquisitive children to follow through with their projects, but have them ask permission to use or purchase the tools necessary to make them happen. These children also may start a process with one idea and find themselves diverted down another road while the first idea is not yet complete, which can be devastating if the experiment is on your kitchen stove! Teach the Aquarian children to stick to one project at a time and to keep notes about the ideas that surface. Then later, they can sift through those ideas and decide which to work on.

The Aquarian children should not be roped in. They need room to test their logic and ideas on the world. Teach them how to do this safely within the spiritual laws. Teach them that the end does not justify the means. These children can get so focused on an idea that they forget everything else around them. They are truly the absent-minded professors. Yes, this is genius, but as a parent, you need to teach them practical skills while still giving them a wide arena to experiment with life.

Health issues for Aquarians involve the calves and ankles. Strength, balance, and flexibility are the keys to health for these children. The strength of their convictions drives them forward, but it takes balance to keep them from losing their foundation in life. And finally, it takes flexibility to change direction when a new understanding is achieved.

Pisces
(February 21–March 20)

The Pisces individual is incredibly sensitive. Piscean Indigos are extremely psychic, too. They have an awareness of past lives even though they don't necessarily understand them. They can have fears due to a psychic impulse or premonition. They need parents to guide them through the shoals of illusion of the lower worlds so that they're not driven to hide from their feelings and psychic intuitions by using substances or engaging in other "aholic" actions.

Pisces children can cry at the drop of a hat. They will latch on to your energy, emotions, and thought patterns before you speak. It's not easy for them to understand traditional schoolwork, because words and actions are a part of the teaching process, which overlooks the importance of kinesthetics. Pisces children are highly kinesthetic and require your insight into this modality in order to successfully mature.

Pisces children need to be nurtured and taught to listen to their feelings. They should keep track of their dreams, and parent should encourage them to discuss them. Parents need to encourage these kids to speak about their inner-world experiences and acknowledge that science does not have all the keys to the soul's true nature.

Give them projects to explore how spirituality and science are coming together. Pisces children love to sleep, read, dream, meditate, and go within. They love fantasy stories, are hopeless romantics, and they originally coined the phrase "and they lived happily ever after." You need to teach them that that phrase refers to the soul, and not experiences in the physical world. In this way, they'll avoid unnecessary bouts of perfectionism and disappointment.

If you do not have the knowledge of traveling the inner worlds and you have a predominantly Pisces children, find them a teacher with integrity who lives by the spiritual laws to teach them. These children need to understand that they're not crazy or "of the devil." However, they experience enlightenment in varying ways and need to be taught what it means.

If there's no one in your area you trust to teach your children in these matters, then sit with them each evening, or at least once a week; and meditate, pray, or listen to an uplifting tape or audio book. When an individual asks for a spiritual teacher and commits to a consistent time each week to learn, the teacher will appear. This does not mean that they'll always appear in a physical form, but oftentimes the learning will come through the meditative, trance, or dream state. Teach Pisces children that their soul comes first, and when they resonate with their heart, they're listening to their soul.

Health issues for Pisces involve the feet. Set a foundation based on spiritual laws, giving them practical techniques to help them safely live in the physical world.

ᘒᘿ *Chapter Thirteen* ᘏᘏ

Unconditional Self-Love

Indigo Children are often perfectionists, and they can be very hard on themselves. They beat themselves up for every perceived infraction. One of the reasons why they become aggressively defensive when you scold them is that they're already painfully aware that they've made a mistake.

Even though Indigos can be maddening at times, it's important to temper how you express your anger toward them. Begin with complimenting them about what they did right before you tell them what they did wrong. Never forget to explain why, and give them reasons for your requests.

Help your children understand that everyone makes mistakes. As *A Course in Miracles* says, "Mistakes require correction, not punishment." So often, Indigo Children feel shame due to their unique qualities, and because they've been told that they're "disordered." Their awkward social skills may cause Indigos to make mistakes when interacting with their friends.

Here are some spiritual healing methods that you can teach your Indigo Children to use whenever they feel that a mistake has been made:

The undoing. When we make a mistake, the effects of that error have a ripple effect. For example, when I was in junior high, I gossiped about a girl. Very soon, the gossip was spread throughout the entire school, and the girl was understandably very hurt and angry. As a result of that event, I learned to keep secrets and avoid gossiping.

So, we Indigo Children may learn valuable lessons from our mistakes, yet we can also learn these lessons without having to suffer. A very effective method for dealing with mistakes is called "The Undoing." This method stops the ripple effects of mistakes from spreading forward. It helps the energy roll backward so that time is unzipped and the energy of the original mistake is undone. The Undoing works, because time is simultaneous instead of linear. Here's how to do it:

The next time your children make a mistake, ask them to say the following:

> *"Dear God, I acknowledge that I have made a mistake, and I ask that all effects of that mistake be undone in all directions in time, for everyone concerned. Thank You."*

Ask your children to sit quietly, breathing deeply, while The Undoing takes place. Share with them anything you felt or saw during the process, and ask them to do the same with you. This method creates miracles! Most likely, the people involved in the argument or misunderstanding will forget why they were upset with your Indigos. They will truly "forgive and forget."

Karma balancing. Sometimes we have problems with people because our soul has a previous history with them. For instance, you might suspect that you've known your Indigo Children in a past life, and you're probably correct. Trust your inner guidance, which will tell you in what way you were previously related to your Indigo Children (mother-daughter, father-son, husband-wife, sister-brother, and so on). Many Indigo Children remember great details about their past lives, and they speak about them matter-of-factly, saying things such as, "Remember when I was the mother and you were the child?" This is especially true with children under the age of five. After that age, many children become more logic based and are less aware of esoteric knowledge.

Whether you believe in past lives or not, you might agree that we carry "karma" in certain relationships. For instance, if you seem to have an ongoing pattern with a certain person, it could be a sign that there's some lesson for you both to learn within the relationship. You and your Indigo Children can balance this karma without having to go through long, arduous, or painful lessons within the relationship by saying to your angels:

> *"I ask that all karma with* (name of person) *be balanced in all directions of time, leaving only the lessons and the love. I am now willing to release any unforgiveness toward* (name of person), *and exchange all pain for peace."*

Sit quietly, and notice any sensations or impressions that come to you. Karma balancing is a powerful process, and most people notice their body shuddering as their cellular memories discharge stored-up energies.

Angel letters. Your children can heal an argument or misunderstanding with someone by contacting the other person's guardian angels. If your Indigo Children are old enough to write, ask them to write a letter to the other person's guardian angels. They can write the letter on paper or on a computer. Anyone can contact someone's guardian angels just by holding the intention of doing so. If your Indigos are too young to write or aren't the writing sort, have them pour their heart out, mentally or aloud, to the other person's guardian angels.

At the end of the communication (whether written, verbal, or mental), your Indigo Children should ask the guardian angels' help in creating a solution. For instance, "I ask your help, angels, in creating peace in this situation. Please help both of us to see the Divine light and love within each other, instead of focusing on fear and darkness. Thank you, angels, for this healing."

Healing Trauma in Indigo Children

When a person endures abuse or some other trauma, the effects can be deep and long-lasting. In a way, we're all trauma survivors. Who among us hasn't been hurt in some way? Yet, there are those who have experienced unimaginable hurt, such as incest, molestation, physical abuse, ritual abuse, or a sudden crime, accident, or loss.

The results of such trauma are often evinced by behavioral and psychological symptoms called posttraumatic stress disorder (PTSD). These symptoms include depression, insomnia or oversleeping, lack of focus, recurring memories or nightmares, feeling unsafe, and difficulty trusting others. Doesn't that sound like some Indigo Child you know?

It could be true that those you know were traumatized in a way you aren't aware of. For instance, many of the girls whom I treated when I was an eating-disorder therapist had suffered trauma during their first sexual encounters. Some were "date raped," and others were manipulated into having sex before they were emotionally ready. But I also feel that life here on Earth is traumatic, period. There are harsh interactions between people, and as one Indigo Child put it, "Kids are really mean to each other."

Bessel van der Kolk, the leading expert on trauma-related PTSD, and author of *Traumatic Stress,* has studied all of the latest scientific research on PTSD. He says that trauma survivors feel disconnected; don't have a clear sense of the present; lack imagination, and have an inability to think of stories. Many trauma survivors become isolated, cynical, and anti-social.

Those with PTSD tend to be emotionally reactive instead of analytical. They react almost exclusively to how they feel, rather than a normal mix of emotions and analytical thought. They also have difficulty thinking their way through problems.

Brain scans on trauma survivors show that their brains behave very differently from those who haven't endured great trauma. For instance, those with PTSD are constantly scanning the horizon and every situation for potential danger. They're always on alert. This can make them seem jumpy and defensive. However, trauma survivors don't notice safe stimuli, so they might miss seeing something that could make them feel happy or safe. If the stimulus isn't dangerous, the person with PTSD doesn't process it because it isn't relevant to their focus. The "amygdala" in the brain (related to noticing stimuli) isn't activated at all in response to nondangerous stimuli.

CAT (brain) scans of those with PTSD were compared to those of people without PTSD. A noise was presented to both individuals, and the people with PTSD showed no response to the noise in their brain's back lobe, where emotions are registered. The non-PTSD control group showed activity in this region. This indicates that the elemental body is numb in those who have PTSD symptoms.

You can help your Indigo Children reawaken their emotional bodies by asking them to take note of examples of happiness or love during the day. Give them rewards for bringing this list home each day. Or, play a game with them by noticing small details when you're both in the car. Van der Kolk says that this method of learning to notice small details is a very effective healing method for those with PTSD.

Van der Kolk also found that there's a difference between reliving and resolving the past trauma. Those who remember the trauma but choose not to talk about it do better psychologically than those who don't remember, or those who talk about it. So don't worry if the Indigo Children you come in contact with don't want to discuss the nature of their past traumas. Van der Kolk has also found that rape survivors heal rapidly by going through a process called "Outward Bound." This experience helps these individuals regain a sense of personal control over their bodies. He also recommends Eye Movement Desensitization and Reprocessing (EMDR) and Somatic Experiencing for survivors of all types of trauma. I've personally witnessed how both of these treatments have helped people heal from the effects of painful memories.

EMDR is a therapeutic process in which the therapist leads the client in a series of eye movements that helps reduce the charge of the traumatic memory. Many studies have shown that not only does EMDR reduce the symptoms of post-traumatic stress disorder, but it also helps the client reframe their traumatic experience so it no longer interferes with their daily functioning. (You can find an EMDR trained therapist through the Website listed in the Resource section of this book.)

Somatic Experiencing (SE) is a body-oriented system of treating trauma that helps the client to gently discharge the frozen physical and emotional memories of the event. Very often, the mind and body become "stuck" at the worst point of the trauma, leaving the person prone to feelings of helplessness and immobility that are often triggered by reminders of the original incident. By thawing the frozen reactions, the person enjoys greater behavioral and emotional flexibility. (A list of SE therapists is available through the Website listed in this book's Resource section.)

Angel Affirmations

Indigo Children feel that they're old souls, and you'll probably agree that this is true. They seem like they're 7 going on 37, and so on. Yet, the Indigos' external maturity may belie their inner insecurities. Many Indigos harbor deep-seated fears about being abandoned if they're "bad." Sadly, many of them feel unworthy of love and will push it away when it's offered. When people emotionally beat themselves up, it can lead to addictions to cover up the inner feelings of inadequacy.

Most Indigos are hungry for positive feelings, even if they seem like tough, I-could-care-less types. I've found that the more difficult someone is to love, the more love that person needs.

Indigo Children know that love is the only truly important part of life. Pam Van Slyke, a special education teacher in Arizona, told me about one example that she witnessed:

> Jason's mom was having a conference with her son's teacher and principal. Jason, age nine, was getting "antsy" while sitting outside the principal's office waiting. He started getting into many things in the administration office that he shouldn't have been touching. I brought him over to a chair where he could see his mom sitting.
>
> Aggravated, after a few seconds, Jason got up and said, "I don't need to do this. I know what's important: I *love* my mom, and my mom *loves* me!" I immediately got goosebumps. Later, I shared the story with Jason's mom. When I was done, tears welled up in her eyes, and she said, "Did he really say that? He *never* tells me anything like that." So, Jason wasn't saying those words like a parrot who mindlessly recites phrases. He apparently really understood that only love matters.

Affirmations can buoy an Indigo Children's sagging self-esteem. Here are some affirmations that you and your children can recite together:

- *I am a holy child of God.*
- *Since God is pure Love, so am I.*
- *I have angels surrounding me now who love me just for who I am.*

- *I can call upon my angels at any time for help, and they are there to help me.*
- *I am unconditionally loved by God and the angels.*
- *I have a lot to offer the world.*
- *My angels can see my hidden talents*
- *I have the power to change the world in important ways*
- *My mind is clear and able to focus perfectly.*
- *I have an infallible photographic memory.*
- *I trust my intuition.*
- *I speak my truth with love and compassion.*
- *I am now working on my Life Purpose, and I feel very fulfilled.*
- *Who I am makes a big difference in this world.*
- *Many people need and love me now.*

꒰ꕤ꒱ ꒰ꕤ꒱ ꒰ꕤ꒱ ꒰ꕤ꒱ ꒰ꕤ꒱ ꒰ꕤ꒱

ᵃ Afterword ᵃ

A Message to Indigo Children

You've chosen a difficult assignment on a difficult planet, but fortunately, you have lots of help available to you. Many of us adults believe in you and what you stand for. We're counting on you to stand by your Life Purpose and not get sidetracked. Every adult needs your collective help—whether they're aware of it or not!

You Indigo Children may be "little lightworkers," yet your Purpose is among the greatest we've experienced on this planet. Your role is essential, even if you're not sure what you're supposed to do yet. By keeping your mind and body attuned with meditation, exercise, communing with nature, and eating healthful foods, you'll be able to clearly understand the Divine guidance that will direct you on your path.

Please don't worry about any perceived deficiencies that you think you might have. If spiritual teachers waited until all their Earthly problems were solved before embarking on their Life Purpose, there wouldn't be any spiritual teachers working on Earth! Everyone has issues, problems, and annoyances to deal with. The trick is to stick to your priorities and not let life's dramas thwart you.

Our lower self—the ego—doesn't want us to work on our Life Purpose. The ego wants us to believe that we're inferior. It wants us to stay stuck and afraid. So it will ask you to hide your Divine light in the name of humbleness, and the ego will have you get busy with meaningless (or less meaningful) tasks, instead of working on your Life Purpose.

Please know that no matter how old you are, you're qualified and ready to help the planet! Any contribution you can make—whether it's sending energy to a troubled person, writing a letter to the editor of a publication, boycotting companies with environmentally unsound products, or donating your allowance to your favorite cause—is appreciated.

Please don't forget how much support you have in the spirit world, Indigo Children! Your team of helpers is waiting for your request right now. Just think the thought, and they'll go to work on your behalf immediately. You don't have to "earn" the help from God or the angels. They see past your surface personality and mistakes, and they see your God-given glory within. The angels are here to enact God's plan of peace, one person at a time. Whatever they can do to help you become more peaceful is a contribution to the entire planet.

Please do your best to resist pressures that could hurt your body or delay your Life Purpose. Ask for a second or third opinion if someone tries to label you with ADD or ADHD. Explore every possible alternative to Ritalin, and do your best to stay away from all drugs, prescription or otherwise.

Remember, we need you! If you delay your Life Purpose, the entire world will be delayed in enjoying peace and health. If life gets frustrating and it seems like others don't understand you, please talk to God or your angels. Try writing your frustrations down on a piece of paper and put the paper in the freezer—that's an excellent method for releasing and surrendering. And many people who use the "freezer method" find that the problems really do get resolved and go away rapidly—and in miraculous ways.

This poem made me cry when I first heard it because it reminded me of you, the precious Indigo Children. I hope that you'll take its words to heart:

My Beloved Children

Break your heart no longer.
Each time you judge yourself,
You break your own heart.
You stop feeding on the Love,
Which is the Wellspring of your Vitality.
The time has come.
Your Time
To Live,
To Celebrate, and
To see the goodness that you are.
You, my Children, are Divine.
You are Pure, and
You are sublimely free.
You are God in disguise, and
You are always perfectly safe.
Do not fight the dark,
Just turn on the Light.
Let Go
And Breathe into the Goodness that you Are.

— Swami Kripalvanandaji

❧❧❧ ❦❦❦

❧ *Bibliography* ❧

Abikoff, H., et al. (1996), "The effects of auditory stimulation on the arithmetic performance of children with ADHD and nondisabled children." *Journal of Learning Disabilities*, 1996 May; 29 (3): pp. 238–246.

Ackerman, C. M., (1997), "Identifying Gifted Adolescents Using Personality Characteristics: Dabrowski's Overexcitabilities." *Roeper Review—A Journal on Gifted Education*, Volume 19, No. 4, June 1997

Amen, Daniel G., M.D. (2001), *Healing ADD*. New York: G. P. Putnam & Sons.

Avanti, Michele. Written interview. For more information, please visit her Website at: **www.Astrologyandmore.com**, or call her at: (775) 673-6568.

Bem, Daryl J. and Honorton, Charles (1994), "Does psi exist? Replicable evidence for an anomalous process of information transfer." *Psychological Bulletin*, Vol. 115, pp. 4–18.

Bhagavan H. N., Coleman, M., Coursin, D.B., (1975), "The effect of pyridoxine hydrochloride on blood serotonin and pyridoxal phosphate contents in hyperactive children," *Pediatrics* 1975 Mar; 55 (3): pp. 437–41.

Bittman, B. B., et al. (2001), "Composite effects of group drumming music therapy on modulation of neuroendocrine-immune parameters in normal subjects." *Alternative Therapy Health Med*. 2001 Jan; 7 (1): pp. 38–47.

Block, Mary Ann, *No More Ritalin: Treating ADHD Without Drugs*. New York: Kensington Publishing Corp., 1996.

Boris, M. and Mandel, F. S. (1994), "Foods and additives are common causes of the attention deficit hyperactive disorder in children." *Ann Allergy* 1994 May; 72 (5): pp. 462–68.

Buchbauer, G., et al. (1991), "Aromatherapy: evidence for sedative effects of the essential oil of lavender after inhalation." *Z Naturforsch* (Germany) [C] 1991 Nov-Dec; 46 (11-12): pp. 1067–72.

Buchbauer, G., et al., (1992), "Effects of valerian root oil, borneol, isoborneol, bornyl acetate and isobornyl acetate on the motility of laboratory animals (mice) after inhalation." *Pharmazie* (Germany)1992 Aug; 47 (8): pp. 620–22.

Butt, M. L. & Kisilevsky, B. S. (2000), "Music modulates behavior of premature infants following heel lance," *Canadian Journal Nurs Res.*, 2000 Mar; 31 (4): pp. 17–39.

Carlton, R. M., et al. (2000), "Rational dosages and learning disabilities," *Alternative Therapies,* Vol. 6, No. 3, May 2000, pp. 85–91.

Coleman M, et al., (1979), "A preliminary study of the effect of pyridoxine administration in a subgroup of hyperkinetic children: a double-blind crossover comparison with methylphenidate." *Biol Psychiatry* 1979 Oct.; 14 (5): pp. 741–51.

Carter, C. M., et al. (1993), "Effects of a few food diet in attention deficit disorder." *Archives Dis Children* 1993 Nov.; 69 (5): pp. 564–68.

Cramond, B. (1995), *"The Coincidence of Attention Deficit Hyperactivity Disorder and Creativity."* The University of Georgia, March 1995, for The National Research Center on the Gifted and Talented.

Dagan, Y., et al. (1997), "Sleep quality in children with attention deficit hyperactivity disorder: an actigraphic study." *Psychiatry Clin Neurosci* 1997 Dec.; 51 (6): pp. 383–86.

Delaveau, P. et al. (1989), "Neuro-depressive properties of essential oil of lavender." *C R Seances Soc Biol Fil* (France), 1989; 183 (4): pp. 342–48

Desor, J. A., et al. (1987), "Longitudinal Changes in Sweet Preferences in Humans." *Physiology and Behavior*, Vol. 39, pp. 639–41.

Desor, J. A., et al. (1973), "Taste in Acceptance of Sugars by Human Infants.*" Journal of Comparative and Physiological Psychology*, Vol. 84, pp. 496–501.

Dey, S., et al. (1992), "Exercise Training: Significance of Regional Alterations in Serotonin Metabolism of Rat Brain in Relation to Antidepressant Effect of Exercise." *Physiology and Behavior*, Vol. 52, No. 6, pp. 1095–99.

Dimeo, F., et al. (2001), "Benefits from aerobic exercise in patients with major depression: a pilot study." *British Journal of Sports Medicine*, 2001 April; 35 (2): pp. 114–17.

Dossey, Larry (1993), *Healing Words: The Power of Prayer and the Practice of Medicine*. New York: Harper Collins.

Dreyfuss, Ira, "Survey: Americans Don't Exercise Enough." Associated Press, Washington, April 1, 2001.

Dyer, J. B. and Crouch, J. G. (1988), "Effects of Running and Other Activities on Moods." *Perceptual and Motor Skills*, Vol. 67, pp. 43–50.

Felthous, Alan R. (1980), "Aggression against cats, dogs, and people," *Children Psychiatry and Human Development* (1980), 10: pp. 169–77.

Freed, Jeffrey and Parsons, Laurie (1997) *Right-Brained Children in a Left-Brained World: Unlocking the Potential of Your ADD Children*. New York: Fireside Publishers.

Goyette, G. H., Connors, C. K., Petti, T. A., Curtis, L. E., (1978), "Effects of artificial colors on hyperkinetic children: a double-blind challenge study." *Psychopharmacol Bull* 1978 Apr; 14 (2): pp. 39–40.

Guillemain J, Rousseau A, Delaveau P. (1989), "Neurodepressive effects of the essential oil of Lavandula angustifolia Mill," *Ann Pharm Fr* (France), 1989; 47 (6): pp. 337–43.

Healy, Jane, M.D. (1991) *Endangered Minds: Why Our Children Don't Think.* New York: Touchstone.

Hirasawam, Y. M., Kawano, K. & Furukawa, A. (1996). "An experiment on extrasensory information transfer with electroencephalogram measurement. *Journal of International Society of Life Information Science*, Vol. 14, pp. 43–48.

Kellert, Stephen R. and Felthous, Alan R., (1983), "Childhood Cruelty Toward Animals Among Criminals and Noncriminals," *Archives of General Psychiatry*, Nov. 1983.

Konofal, E., Lecendreux, M., Bouvard, M. P., & Mouren-Simeoni, M. C. (2001), "High levels of nocturnal activity in children with attention-deficit hyperactivity disorder: a video analysis." *Psychiatry Clin Neurosci* 2001 Apr.; 55 (2): pp. 97–103.

Kozielec, T., Starobrat-Hermelin. B., Kotkowiak, L., (1994), "Deficiency of certain trace elements in children with hyperactivity," *Psychiatr Pol* 1994, May-June; 28 (3): pp. 345–53.

Kozielec, T., Starobrat-Hermelin, B., (1997), "Assessment of magnesium levels in children with attention deficit hyperactivity disorder (ADHD)," *Magnes Res* 1997, June; 10 (2): pp. 143–48.

Lad, Vasant, (1984), "*Aryurveda: The Science of Self Healing.*" Wilmot, WI: Lotus Press.

Lou, Hans, et al. "Focal Cerebral Dysfunction in Developmental Learning Disabilities." *The Lancet*, January 6, 1990.

MacDonald, W. L. (1995), "The effects of religiosity and structural strain on reported paranormal experiences." *Journal for the Scientific Study of Religion*, Vol. 34, pp. 366–76.

McCann, I. L. and Holmes, D. S. (1984), "Influence of Aerobic Exercise on Depression." *Journal of Personality and Social Psychology*, Vol. 46, No. 5, pp. 1142–47.

Mitchell, E. A., et al. (1987), "Clinical characteristics and serum essential fatty acid levels in hyperactive children," *Clinical Pediatrics,* 26 (1987): pp. 406–11.

Morningstar, Amadea (1990). *The Ayurvedic Cookbook: A Personalized Guide to Good Nutrition and Health.* Twin Lakes, WI: Lotus Press.

Norton, Amy. "Exercise Beats Drugs for Some with Depression." *Reuters Health News*, March 27, 2001.

Pinchasov, B. B., et al. (2000), "Mood and energy regulation in seasonal and non-seasonal depression, before and after midday treatment with physical exercise or bright light." *Psychiatry Res.* 2000, April 24; 94 (1): pp. 29–42.

Potteiger, J. A., Schroeder, J. M., and Goff, K. L. (2000),"Influence of music on ratings of perceived exertion during 20 minutes of moderate intensity exercise." *Percept Motor Skills* 2000 Dec; 91 (3 Pt 1): pp. 848–54.

Quider, R. F. (1984), "The effect of relaxation/suggestion and music on forced-choice ESP scoring. *Journal of the American Society for Pyschical Research*, Vol. 78, pp. 241–62.

Radin, Dean I. (1996), "Silent shockwaves: Evidence for presentiment of emotional futures." *European Journal of Parapsychology*, Vol. 12.

Reid, Daniel (1989) *The Tao of Health, Sex, and Longevity: A Modern Practical Guide to the Ancient Way*. New York: Fireside Publishers.

Robotham, Julie, "In 2001, It's Readin', Writin', and Ritalin." *The Sydney Morning Herald*, March 19, 2001, p. A-1.

Robson, W. L., et al. (1997), "Enuresis in children with attention-deficit hyperactivity disorder." *South Med J* 1997 May; 90 (5): pp. 503–5.

Rose, T. L., (1978), "The functional relationship between artificial food colors and hyperactivity," *Journal of Appl Behav Anal* 1978 Winter; 11 (4): pp. 439–46

Rowe, K. S., (1988), "Synthetic food colourings and 'hyperactivity': a double-blind crossover study," *Australia Paediatric Journal,* April 1988, Vol. 24 (2), pp. 143–47.

Rowe, K. S. & Rowe, K. J. (1994), "Synthetic food coloring and behavior: a dose response effect in a double-blind, placebo-controlled, repeated-measures study." *Journal of Pediatrics,* November 1994, Vol. 135, pp. 691–98.

Schoenthaler, S. J. & Bier, I. D. (2000), "The effect of vitamin-mineral supplementation on juvenile delinquency among American schoolchildren: a randomized, double-blind placebo-controlled trial," *Journal of Alternative and Complementary Medicine, Vol. 6,* No. 1, February 2000, pp. 7–17.

Schoenthaler, S. J., et al. (1986), "The Testing of Various Hypotheses as Explanations for the Gains in National Standardized Academic Test Scores in the 1978-1983 New York City Nutrition Policy Modification Project," *International Journal of Biosocial Research*, Vol. 8 (2), pp. 196–03.

Schoenthaler, S. J. (1985), "Institutional Nutritional Policies and Criminal Behavior," *Nutrition Today*, 20(3), 1985, pp. 25–39.

————— (1983), "Diet and Crime: An Empirical Examination of the Value of Nutrition in the Control and Treatment of Incarcerated Juvenile Offenders," *International Journal of Biosocial Research*, 4(1), 1983, pp. 25–39.

————— (1983), "Types of Offenses Which Can Be Reduced in an Institutional Setting Using Nutritional Intervention: A Preliminary Empirical Evaluation," *International Journal of Biosocial Research*, 4(2), 1983, pp. 74–84.

————— (1983), "The Los Angeles Probation Department Diet Behavior Program: An Empirical Evaluation of Six Institutions," *International Journal of Biosocial Research*, 5 (2), 1983, p. 88.

————— (1983), "The Northern California Diet-Behavior Program: An Empirical

Examination of 3,000 Incarcerated Juveniles in Stanislaus County Juvenile Hall," *International Journal of Biosocial Research*, 5 (2), 1983, pp. 99–106.

Starobrat-Hermelin, B., Kozielec, T., (1997), "The effects of magnesium physiological supplementation on hyperactivity in children with attention deficit disorder (ADHD): Positive response to magnesium oral loading test." *Magnes Res* 1997 Jun; 10 (2): pp. 149–56.

Stevens, Laura J. (2000), *12 Effective Ways to Help Your ADD/ADHD Children*. New York: Penguin Putnam, Inc.

Swanson, J. & Kinsbourne, M. (1980), "Food Dyes Impair Performance of Hyperactive Children on a Laboratory Learning Test," *Science* magazine, March 28, 1980, Vol. 207. pp. 1485–87.

Tappe, Nancy (1982), *Understanding Your Life Through Color*. Carlsbad, CA: Starling Productions. This book is not widely distributed. To obtain, call Awakening Book Store in California (949) 457-0797, or Mind, Body, Soul Bookstore in Indiana, pp. 889–3612.

USA Today (March 15, 2001, p. 8D). "Poll: Kids Worry About School Violence."

Washington Times, June 23, 1998. "Animal Cruelty May Be a Warning."

Virtue, D. L., *Constant Craving: What Your Food Cravings Mean and How to Overcome Them*. Carlsbad, CA: Hay House, 1995.

Weeks, David. *Eccentrics: The Scientific Investigation* (Stirling University Press, 1988).

Zale, Gabrielle, Written interview. For more information, Gabrielle's Website is: www.littlelights.com.

❦❧❦❧❦❧ ❧❦❧❦❧❦

✶ Resources ✶

Astrology by Michele Avanti. For more information, please visit her Website at: **www.Astrologyandmore.com**, or call her at: (775) 673-6568.

EarthSave International: Leads a global movement of people from all walks of life who are taking concrete steps to promote healthy and life-sustaining food choices. EarthSave supplies information, support, and practical programs to those who have learned that their food choices impact environmental and human health. Many local chapters have active social and singles clubs. Website: **earthsave.org** • Phone: (831) 423-0293 • Fax: (831) 423-1313 • (800) 362-3648 (toll-free).

Eye Movement, Desensitization, and Reprocessing (EMDR). Gives information about EMDR trauma therapy, and a list of EMDR-trained therapists. Website: **www.emdria.com**

Foundation for Human Enrichment. A resource for finding information on Somatic Experiencing (SE) and a list of SE practitioners. Website: **www.fhe.com**

Gaiam: An Internet shopping site where you can buy healthful foods and Earth-friendly products on-line. Gaiam is linked with Whole Foods Market, enabling you to purchase their items from the Internet. Website: **www.gaiam.com**

Green Market Place: "Environmentally Friendly Foods and Products." This Website allows you to purchase nontoxic, organic, and recycled household products, including cleaning supplies, paper products, and toiletries. Website: **greenmarketplace.com** • Phone: (888) 59-EARTH.

Kids and Organics: A great site for kids of all ages, explaining the ABC's of organic farming and eating. Website: **www.kids.organics.org/Organic/organic.htm.**

Psychic Kids: A Website for and about psychic children: **www.psykids.net**

Waldorf Schools. Based on Austrian philosopher Rudolf Steiner's holistic approach to schooling, these educational facilities promote emotional, physical, spiritual, and intellectual growth in their students. ADD/ADHD is virtually nonexistent in Waldorf students. Information: 3911 Bannister Rd., Fair Oaks, CA 95628. Phone: (916) 961-0927 • Fax: (916) 961-0715 • Website: **www.awsna.org/**

✶✶✶ ✶✶✶

✤ *About the Author* ✤

Doreen Virtue, Ph.D., is a spiritual doctor of psychology and a contributing author of the book *The Indigo Children*. The mother of four Indigo Children (which includes stepdaughters), she has extensive personal and professional experience with "Little Lightworkers," as she calls them. Doreen is the author of numerous spiritual self-help books, tapes, and oracle cards, including *Healing with the Angels; Angel Therapy*; and *The Lightworker's Way*.

Doreen is a frequent talk-show guest, with appearances on *Oprah*, CNN, *Good Morning America, The View with Barbara Walters,* and other programs. Her work has been featured in *Glamour, Redbook, Woman's Day, Cosmopolitan, Fitness,* and other magazines and newspapers.

Doreen gives workshops around the world on topics related to her books and tapes. For information on her seminars and her other books, please visit her Website at: **AngelTherapy.com**

✤✤✤ ✤✤✤

Other Hay House Titles
of Related Interest

We hope you enjoyed
this Hay House book.
If you would like to receive a free catalog
featuring additional Hay House books and products,
or if you would like information about the
Hay Foundation, please contact:

Hay House, Inc.
P.O. Box 5100
Carlsbad, CA 92018-5100

(760) 431-7695 or (800) 654-5126
(760) 431-6948 (fax) or (800) 650-5115 (fax)

Please visit the Hay House Website at:
www.hayhouse.com

❧❧❧ ❦❦❦